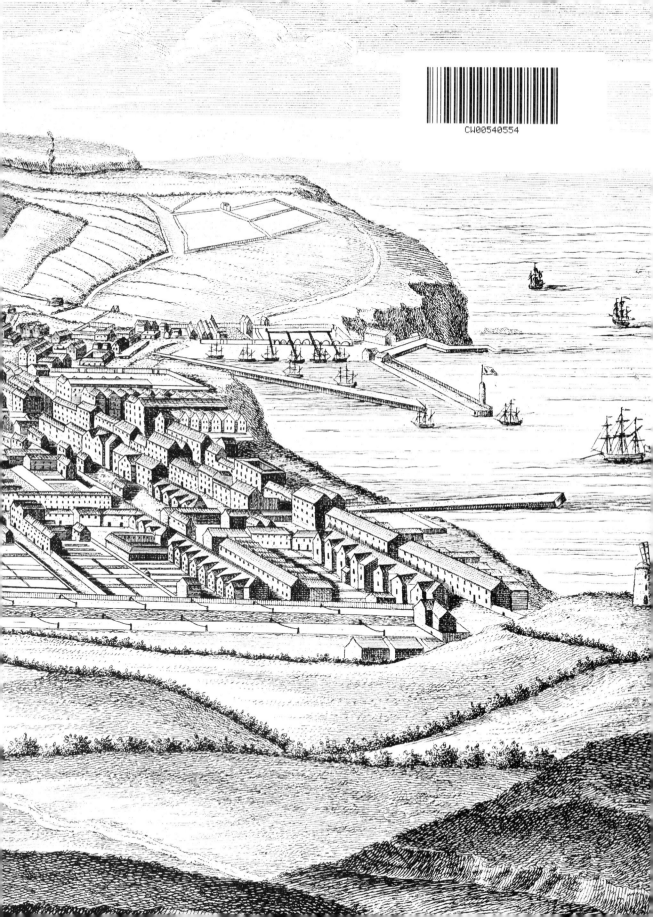

READ'S POINT OF VIEW

READ'S POINT OF VIEW

Paintings of the Cumbrian Countryside

MATHIAS READ

1669 – 1747

by

Mary E. Burkett and David Sloss

SKIDDAW PRESS

1995

ISBN 0 900811 285

Printed by Titus Wilson, Kendal

To the memory of the late Daniel Hay of Whitehaven.

"Streit mine eye has caught new pleasures
Whilst the landskip round it measures"

John Milton. *L'Allegro*

ACKNOWLEDGEMENTS

The compilation of this work has been carried out over a number of years and many people have helped.

The first serious study of Read in the twentieth century was made by the late Daniel Hay who was librarian at Whitehaven for many years. Sincere gratitude is accorded to Denis Perriam for use of a paper he wrote on the artist a few years ago and for advice on the text. Grateful acknowledgements are due to Mr & Mrs Leslie Black, Leslie Randall and Lucy Sclater for photographing most of the works.

Information has been given by Pamela Dickinson, Michael Moon, Michael Bottomley, Harry Fancy and Audrey Hartland, who helped to identify some sites and objects portrayed in the pictures. Thanks also go to Nigel Harris for the information on country pursuits. Much gratitude goes to our good friend from America, L. Kirkby of Claremount for finding the location of the Boar Hunt by Sawrey Gilpin.

Assistance in preparing the manuscript has been given initially by Lady Moon and subsequently by Dorathy Morgan who has unstintingly typed and retyped the text over the last two years.

We wish to thank the owners sincerely for their collaboration and kindness. Not only did they tolerate our frequent invasion of their privacy but entered into the research with enthusiasm.

Finally we could not have published without financial help from The Paul Mellon Centre for Studies in British Art, the Marc Fitch Fund, Christopher Foley of Lane Fine Art Ltd., and for further help towards the photography David McDowall, Christies and Phillips.

M.E.B,

D.S.

1995

CONTENTS

COLOURED PLATES

(between pp. 16 and 17)

BLACK AND WHITE ILLUSTRATIONS

Endpapers: detail of Richard Parr's print of Whitehaven.

PREFACE

In Britain there is a venerable tradition for an interest in local history and the affairs of a region. Antiquity and antiquarianism have been subjects of enquiry for more than four hundred years. The compilation of county histories has been a quintessentially national vocation. For this very reason our county record offices are the best in the world. We might encapsulate all this by mention of the Society of Antiquaries. As a London institution it might be said to have spawned many a local antiquarian and historical society, or more idiosyncratic conviviums such as the Spalding Gentlemen's Society. If these societies were earlier focuses of local studies, today these are often centred in the provincial, or what we now call, regional museums. Such a one is the Abbot Hall Art Gallery at Kendal, first formed by the Lake District Gallery Trust in 1957 and officially opened in Abbot Hall in 1962. In 1966 Miss Mary Burkett became Director, and from then, until she retired in 1986, the artistic and historical affairs of Cumbria have been synonymous with her name.

I may claim a certain affinity with Mary, because we have both been centrifugal forces for exactly the same period of time in our respective institutions, and I find a letter written to her as early as 1965. What one recognized in her then was a museum curator and historian deeply knowledgeable of her locality, but also a collector keen to enliven Abbot Hall with appropriate acquisitions, notably portraiture, often related to the local Cumbrian scene; and so, in came George Romney's great portrait group of the Gower Family in 1974 or the munificent purchase of fifty-nine paintings from the Hothfield Collection in 1981, that included the Great Picture of Lady Anne Clifford, surely one of the icons of English portrait art.

Whenever I wrote to Mary, it always elicited a prompt and intelligent response. I could have wished for no better, when in 1977 I enquired about Mathias Read (1669-1747) for my book *The Artist and the Country House*. Like John Setterington of Scarborough, Read seems to have confined himself to this county. He was the artistic factotum of the Lowthers of Whitehaven and Lowther Castle. It can hardly be a coincidence that Read was reputed to have been involved with the Irish troubles in 1689 - 1690, and to have made copies of paintings by Jan Wyck, who had painted William III crossing the Boyne and the Battle of the Boyne for Sir John Lowther in 1690 and a view of Whitehaven from the sea in 1686. The connection between Wyck and Read, probably as master and pupil, can hardly be doubted, for when Wyck died in 1702, Read seems to have succeeded him in the Lowther's patronage. Perhaps it was a case of the local young painter making good.

In Cumbria Read is the chief limner in paint on canvas of the local scene. In a sense, we can visualise his presence dominating the artistic affairs of Whitehaven, especially after 1702 when he married a local girl. He must have been in charge of all the painterly tasks at the Lowther's various houses, perhaps even acting as a curator of their pictures. His masterpiece of topography is undoubtedly the huge prospect of Whitehaven, of which several versions exist, one dated 1733 and one engraved in 1738. No other English town has been so well surveyed in paint, and in this alone Read of Whitehaven can take his place among the metropolitan topographers.

There are fruitful ramifications from the Lowther's patronage. Both Kneller and Tillemans must have known Read, and when William Gilpin (1650-1724) of Scaleby Castle commissioned paintings and received tuition in drawing and painting from Read, the consequences upon Gilpin's grandson, the famous William Gilpin of Picturesque Theory, would then not have been suspected. However, for anyone looking at those chiaroscuro acquatint views by the grandson, there is surely a stylistic connection returning to Read of Whitehaven.

In 1976 Mary Burkett wrote of her ambitions for Read. Now, nearly twenty years on a book has been written, and Read has been given the attention in the affairs of Whitehaven that he so well deserves. For this we must not only thank Mary Burkett but her able friend and colleague David Sloss. It would be appropriate that Read's Exhibition, *Point of View, Paintings of the Cumbria Countryside*, should be held in Abbot Hall, but it must be seen as the latest in an exhibitions programme that sets Abbot Hall quite apart from many other of the smaller regional museums. Mary and David have now commemorated Read, as they did William Green of Ambleside in 1984, and for my own architectural interests I recollect that excellent work on the Websters of Kendal. Looking at that long and impressive list of Mary Burkett's achievements, some may be surprized to find exhibitions devoted to Persian art, or the Turcoman of Iran and the Art of the Felt Maker. The answer is that Mary Burkett is the recognised authority on oriental felt.

Cumbria without Mary Burkett would have been a poorer place. She made Abbot Hall a power house of the localilty. Of course, this is not an obituary, for she is still with us, and will continue to enrich the artistic and historical affairs of the Lake District and around. It is also appropriate that she is now the chatelaine of Isel Hall, and can observe the well being of Abbot Hall from that lovely and romantic castle.

JOHN HARRIS

The South East Prospect
of Whitehaven in the Year 1642.

1. *The Chapel.*   3. *The Rope Walks.*
2. *The Harbour.*   4. *Part of Scotland.*

1   Early engraving of Whitehaven c.1642

CHAPTER 1

WHY WHITEHAVEN?

There is an engraving of **The South East Prospect of Whitehaven in the Year 1642** showing a tiny hamlet not far from the bay.[1] To the east lay the mountains of the Lake District long before the tourist trade began in the eighteenth century. Indeed early visitors such as Celia Fiennes, Daniel Defoe and even Camden described the area as some of the wildest, most barren and frightful in the whole country. The print shows the hills sloping gently down to the sea and the small community was sheltered by cliffs to the south and the north. What changed the fate of this small community and indeed a large area surrounding it, was the activity of one indigenous entrepreneurial landed family – the Lowthers.

Originally from the Manor of St Bees, Sir Christopher, but mainly his son Sir John Lowther (1642-1706) 2nd baronet and his son Sir James (1673-1755), set about systematically acquiring more and more land. He was developing and exploiting the main resource of his estates, coal. But Sir John was not merely an entrepreneur. Commercial though he undoubtedly was, he was also an idealist and a philanthropist. He described himself as "a man of business, with an estate not to be improved and preserved without pains and care".[2] He was public spirited and concerned for the welfare of all, including the poor. The immense volume of letters between Sir John and his agent Gilpin is evidence of his enthusiasm and interest in the aesthetic enhancement of his collection of properties. It is to be remembered that no less a figure than Kneller advised him on his painting collections.

His son James inherited many of his father's traits and in 1726 sponsored a bill in the House of Commons "to hinder the poor people from being starved by people that harass and oppress them".[3]

Whitehaven became the "earliest post-mediaeval planned town in England".[4]

It is hard to imagine now that Whitehaven was once a thriving trading centre equal to Liverpool, Bristol and Glasgow, but so it became under the zeal of the Lowther family from their chief seat Flatt Hall, bought from Sir John Fletcher of Hutton-in-the-Forest in 1675. In 1736 Lowther was using 100 ships in his rapidly expanding coal trade, and 87,000 tons were exported that year. By 1750 his collieries were producing 170,000 tons and mainly because of his activities Workington and Maryport were also thriving ports. Apart from trade in coal, tobacco and salt, there was a flourishing agricultural market. Schools were being established early in the eighteenth century; chapels and churches were built to encourage all Christian Sects – Presbyterians, Seceders, Anabaptists, Quakers as well as Church of England and Roman Catholics.

"Houses were built for merchants and poor people".[5] Today a few original details appear in the windows, doorways, the fine symmetry of facades, and elevations. There are still some lovely stairways inside, elegant plaster work, alcoves and Dutch tiles. The size, proportions and building materials were carefully planned and controlled. It was an orderly development allowing for private enterprise and originality. There was a newspaper as early as 1736. Amusements such as cockfighting, bowls, a playhouse and "An assembly room for the diversion of the Ladies" were introduced.[6]

With this development there was an explosive rise in population, which resulted in the usual problems of the developing industrial centres; food shortages, unemployment and epidemics. Aware of these problems Sir John introduced a hospital and medical care.

Sir John Lowther's vision for Whitehaven was an imaginative one. The central road running west-east went from the harbour to Flatt Hall. It was called Lowther Street and reserved for buildings "above the ordinary". To the north and south running parallel to it, Duke and Roper Streets, and crossing these at right angles were four lesser streets. Everything was carried out in an orderly way and plots were planned and could be bought by anyone who wished to settle. He and his son also gave grants to those who could not afford to buy. He wished to "be a builder at Whitehaven, not for any profit, being even content to sustain some loss, but rather to draw people thither". Also he said he wished to ensure "that newcomers may never want a place to receive them".[7] Sir James Lowther said later – 1753 – "people are mad to give such prices for small parcels of land as they do in Cumberland, they don't give such near London".

Certainly there had been idealism in the design of Whitehaven resulting in T. Pennant's remark in 1772 "one of the handsomest towns in the North of England".[8] Sir John himself thought its orderly development had succeeded, though he was not an emotional man, he said it was "one of the prettiest towns in England". In 1751 Sir James commented "the town has got as near my house as I ever thought I'd let them come in my time". It is true that the spaces had to be sacrificed for the growing number of people who wanted to live in the town. The first concept had, however, taken fully into account the impact of architecture on the landscape.

Landscape, and architecture in the landscape, were viewed with new eyes. Large houses, estates, small country cottages, bridges, churches and monastic sites, ruins and follies all came under the close scrutiny of the artist with pencil, paint, brush and pen.

By 1800, however, it was all to change again. The national economy went into recession, and the silting-up of the port of Whitehaven contributed to its decline.

CHAPTER 2

MATHIAS READ'S INTRODUCTION INTO
THE AREA

It is extremely difficult to find documentary evidence on Mathias Read. Records show that he was born at Clerkenwell, London of William Rede (Read) and Hannah Blount in 1669. According to the historian Hutchinson, Mathias Read had come to Whitehaven sometime about 1690 from Ireland where he had been employed by a naval sea captain of King William's Fleet during the Battle of the Boyne.[9]

Tradition holds that he went to Ireland originally with Jan Van Wyck, (1652-1702) as his pupil. Certainly on the way back from Ireland when Wyck arrived at Whitehaven, Sir John Lowther commissioned the latter to paint a landscape view of Whitehaven taken from the entrance to the harbour, also in 1690 to paint a portrait of **William III crossing the Boyne** and a picture of the **Battle of the Boyne**.[10,11]

William III took great pains to encourage artists from his own country to come to England and preferably to settle in London. Many of them covered the wars in Ireland of 1688. This is what led Jan Van Wyck to go there. Probably Read would have had plenty of practice filling in the landscapes while Wyck painted the people in the battle scenes. This may partly explain why it took time for Read to establish a reputation in Whitehaven. It was through painting portraits that artists were esteemed the most.

William Gilpin (1650-1724) who had been employed by Sir John Lowther of Whitehaven was made Recorder of Carlisle. Gilpin says in a letter to Sir John Lowther dated 10 May 1693, "Here is a young man now in town, who is painting the roof of the church in fretwork (which he does well) but his trade is carving. He offers to do the carved work of your seat in antique and fruitage, to be wrought on both sides, for 8s a foot, or cheaper if any workman in London will undertake it cheaper. I am satisfied that he will design it well, and draw it truly – and I think he may be employed in it".[12]

In early 1694 Gilpin paid the anonymous carver a total of £13.8s for carving 33½ feet of border for Lowther's pew and 12s extra for carving two "modilions" with £1.14s to the painter for fitting the carved work, and varnishing and painting the pew in imitation of "Batick Oak".[13] It is almost certain that this painter was Mathias Read. No sign of the work remains today.

" 15 Feb'y 1693 – To the Carver in part for Carving
                       the Border about Sir John Lowther's
                       seat in the New Church at Whitehaven   2   –   –
     15 Mar 1693 – More to the Carver of Sir John
                       Lowther's seat   4   –   –
     25 Mar 1694 – To the Carver £7.8.0 Cro.ch with £2 paid
                       him at fol 18 and £1 and £3 at fol makes
                       £13.8.7 in full for 3½ foot Carved Work
                       at 8shlgs per foot, for the Border of Sir
                       Lowther's Seat, in the Church at
                       Whitehaven   £7   8   0
                  – To Do. more carving two Modilions   –   12   –
                  – To the Painter for varnishing the
                       Carv'd work & painting the seal in
                       Imitation of Ballick Oak £1.10.0 and
                       paid more for Cutting the plank, and
                       for fitting the Carv'd work   £1   14   –" [14]

Later in 1695 he says "the painter in town, though no Raphael, deserves encouragement. He has a good fancy, and is capable of direction. I have commissioned him to do several pieces when he was under discouragement, and approve his performances, and would be sorry, for Whitehaven's sake, to see him quit the town". In a third letter of 2 Feb 1697/8 "But the painter does improve not only in colouring, but in drawing also, to that degree that I have hopes he may prove to be a good designer".

His early life was probably difficult but he received great support from Gilpin and through him, Sir John Lowther.

We understand also from the Lowther papers that Sir Godfrey Kneller had first drawn Sir John's attention to Jan Wyck. Among the portraits of the Lowther family in their Whitehaven house, Flatt Hall, later renamed Lowther Hall, were several painted by Kneller. Read and Wyck, in whatever way they had met, are likely to have worked together for some time until Wyck died in 1702. Another interesting aspect of this little coterie is that Kneller actually painted a portrait of Jan Van Wyck. He also acted as advisor to Sir John Lowther in building up his collection of pictures for all his houses. The bulk of these were Dutch and Italian Masters but there were a number of Kneller's own portraits in this collection. Later Read was commissioned in turn to copy these portraits – "five copies after Kneller" – were still in the Flatt in 1757. Read also copied Snyder's **Reynard triumphant** which was in the Lowther Collection.[15] Sir John Lowther employed Read in a number of ways one being "to paint some historical pieces in the apartments of the Flatt". No doubt such patronage helped towards his success in Whitehaven, as we are told "His productions there excited a strong desire in the principal inhabitants to have his pencil employed in some suitable ornament for their new chapel . . ."[16]

In the seventeenth century it was still quite customary for artists to be obliged to undertake painting of any sort. "Last night painted the ceiling of great drawing room – today portrait of Mr Hasell . . ."[17] describes an episode in the career of an earlier Cumbrian artist, Thomas Webster in 1696.

Looked at in the wider European context it is interesting to see historic parallels. Eliane Gondinet Wallstein[18] relates

"Van Eyck, van der Weyden, ne sont pas considérés comme de grands personnages dont la vie mériterait, par exemple, d'être rapportée par les choniquers de la cour de Bourgogne. Ils sont plutôt des artisans "peintres d'images", dont l'atelier reçoit toutes sortes de commandes: Décoration de murs, de meubles, d'armures; peintures d'écussons, d'étendards, de bannières de procession . . . Ils font les toiles peintes qui servent de décor aux mystères, collaborent à la mise en scène des "joyeuses entrées" du duc en ses villes de Flandre ou de Bourgogne; ils polychroment les statues exécutées par leur confrères sculpteurs . . . leurs travaux sont rémunérés sur la base du temps d'exécution, non sur celle de la valeur artistique, et la plupart du temps ils ne sont signés."

Again from **The Merchant of Prato** by Iris Origo (Cape 1857.) "During the trecento in Tuscany, the price of the picture usually depended on its size. A large painting took more time and used more expensive materials, as gold and azzuro transmarino, prepared from lapis lazuli. We learn from the correspondence of Francesco Datini, by 1390 an important and very rich merchant in both Florence and Prato, that he was recommended two painters. "One of them was a saddler by trade, the other a painter who carves figures". No hard and fast line divided the craftsman from the artist: a dipintore would not disdain to pass from painting a sacred altar-piece to distempering the walls of a house, or to the decoration of chests, curtains, shields and banners, or to saddle-cloths and harness, of waxen figures or earthenware bowls. Arrigo di Niccolo dipintore, who painted one of the panels which Francesco presented to the church, also distempered and decorated the walls of his courtyard and of his warehouse – and was paid at much the same rate for both services."

The extent and diverse nature of jobs undertaken by Read over the years may be seen in the following entries in the Lonsdale papers:

Cash Book:

2 Nov 1696:	To ye Painter for Colouring the great Gate & other doors & woodwork in Oyl colour as yr Note – – – – – – – – – – –	1	15	8
29th July 1710	To ret'd by Mr Read from Mr Lowther upon my letter	5	–	–
7th Sept 1710	To be returned by Mr Read for making of yr Sheriff's Livery	–	2	6

John Spedding, Estate Steward to James Lowther, wrote from White-haven on 14 May 1721: "I should be glad to know if you would have the pictures hung up again in the Gallery, & or you will let it alone till you come down. Many of 'em want to be cleaned & washed or varnisht over, wen Mr Read tells me he will be very ready to give his best Assistance in – – –"

J. Spedding to J. Lowther (Sir James). Whitehaven, 26 May 1731: "Mr Read has painted the parlour and dining room (at Flatt Hall) and they look very well".

Spedding to Lowther, Whitehaven, 25 June 1732: "Mr Read has painted the new room over the Brewhouse and everything else is finished about the House. (Flatt Hall)"[19]

Among the Lonsdale papers are the Saltom Colliery Records of Christmas Quarter 1731 which reveal that this was still the case. "Mr Read painting the engine – 19s 4d" (one of the engines in the new pits). Included in the same records, "Charge of Saltom Pitt Begun 4th March 1729". [20, 21]

However he did not only paint engines. Another source of information is in the writings of the Reverend William Gilpin, rector of Boldre, a grandson of William Gilpin, and well known for his works on aesthetics and the picturesque. From him comes another insight into the various jobs Read had to carry out, "At Whitehaven lived a painter of little note, where nothing could be less esteemed than his art. He wrought cheap, and was employed chiefly in daubing colours on the heads and sterns of ships".[22] His efforts were all worthwhile however, as Gilpin writes later:- "Read became celebrated for his abilities, and business flowed in upon him so abundantly, that he was induced to settle in the town; and, in the course of a long life (he died at 78) he painted more, perhaps, than any other artist in his time . . ." "He busied Read in the painting of landscapes, portrait, and history. It appears that in the last two branches he (Read) had no great quality." "But where he had easy nature before him, he was often happy in his imitations. Tho' he knew nothing of the artificial composition of landscape, he touched a tree, or a piece of foreground, with spirit; and in flower-pieces he rather excelled".[23] It is not necessarily to his detriment that Read was criticized for his lack of "artificial composition of landscape".

It is tantalizing to think that so far in the present researches only 50 actual examples of his work have been found, another five are thought to have perished and no doubt a great many lie unattributed to him or are thought to be by a variety of other artists. Many may have gone abroad, and some may still be on panels, covered up with layers of paint, in the remaining early houses of the area.

2 Mathias Read's house as it is today

In 1875 William Jackson[24] a Whitehaven writer said "A painting on panel over the chimney-piece in the back bedroom in a house is by Read". He does not mention whether this was Mathias Read's house but gives the address as Cross Street. The picture represents Judith handing the head of Holofernes to her female attendant. " Owing to the disagreeable nature of the subject, which met the owner's eye every morning when he awoke, it was doomed to destruction many years ago; but out of deference to the much respected brother of the brush, long ago deceased, who was requested to obliterate it with another coat of paint, it was spared for time to throw his consuming shadows on it". After much searching in the house no trace can be found of this now. In another house in Cooper's Court, Quay Street, a panel was known to have been painted over the fireplace on the left of the entrance door. It was of Egremont Castle and almost erased when last referred to.[25] It had been the property of Dr Joshua Dixon a well known benefactor of the town, and patron of the infirmary. When visited recently the site which used to be, according to the 1792 map of Whitehaven, known as 5 Quay Street – there was no longer the courtyard, the road, or even the house, let alone the panel. Such has been the devastation of early buildings in Whitehaven in this century, that many other pictures must have suffered the same fate.

Through meeting Sir John's agent William Gilpin (1650-1724) Read had ample opportunity to visit Scaleby Castle, near Irthington and study the pictures there. Gilpin and Read certainly seem to have struck up a friend-ship straightaway and Gilpin admired his work enough to ask Read to teach him the elements of drawing and painting. Mr Gilpin noticing that he had been painting ships' sterns "easily saw he had genius above such employment". It did not rest there, Read went on to teach Gilpin's son John Bernard (1701-1776) who was so enthusiastic that he even contemplated taking up art as a profession. Instead however he made his career as a soldier. He in turn encouraged his two sons William and Sawrey, who both made their names in the art world. William, as well as painting, was the author of "Remarks in Forest Scenery & other Woodland Views (relating chiefly to picturesque beauty, illustrated in the scene of the New Forest) and 'Observations relative to Picturesque Beauty, made in the year 1772 on several parts of England, particularly the mountains and lakes of Cumberland and Westmorland (2 Vols 1786)", and many other similar books. His brother Sawrey was at first destined to be a marine artist but his talents lay not in the depiction of ships but of horses. His work has become increasingly well known and is represented in galleries and collections throughout the world. Mr Hay believed all this stemmed from Read's strong influence on their grandfather.

It was in fact Captain J. B. Gilpin who taught George Hoare, Guy Head, Robert Smirke, Joseph Stephenson and Dr. John Brown, who wrote one of the first descriptions of Derwentwater.[26] Indeed John Warwick Smith's father was gardener to the Captain's sister. Warwick Smith was sent by the Captain to St. Bees School and then to a drawing master near Whitehaven – later he was apprenticed in London to Sawrey Gilpin. Read's nephew Joseph Hinde cannot help but have been influenced by Read. It's no exaggeration to say that the Rev. Gilpin's writings on the picturesque were influential and very widely read at the end of the 18th century and provoked much subsequent discussion on the aesthetic of landscape painting.

As the years passed so Read's popularity grew; and his work was increasingly in great demand. William Gilpin said "There was hardly a house in Whitehaven whose master could afford it, which had not a picture or two painted on panels over doors or chimneys by his hand." This fact has proved no exaggeration as panels found in researches have extended to places up to twelve miles from Whitehaven and paintings on canvas far further afield.

Such was his success in Whitehaven that he settled there permanently. Land was conveyed to him in 1701[27] and he built a fair sized house, 5 Cross Street. The exact location of Read's house in Whitehaven appeared at first to be a mystery. From a study of the various street directories of Whitehaven, it appears that he lived in both Irish Street and Cross Street from 1713 until his death. This can easily be resolved by the suggestion that Read built his own house in 1713 at the corner of both streets. From the same street directories we find that in 1728 Read is referred to for the first time as Mr Read, at a time when that title was only given to gentlemen of some standing. It is evident he had become, "notwithstanding his education having been somewhat inferior, for his hand-writing bears that stamp, a man of some consideration".[28]

On 17th May 1702, the St Nicholas Church Marriage Register records his marriage to a local girl Elizabeth Hinde. She was the daughter of Leonard Hinde originally of Preston. On 5th June 1703 their son William was born, then two years later on 13th July 1705 their first daughter Jane, finally on 4th April 1707 their third child Elizabeth. Alas only Elizabeth survived. She married and the family continued. William died in 1724 at 21 and Jane died still in her teens.

In Lowther Street there used to be a chapel. This was replaced by St Nicholas Church which was consecrated in 1693 and completely rebuilt in 1708 to house the ever increasing population of Whitehaven.[29] Restoration was spearheaded by Elisha Gale a member of a family who had been for years second to the Lowthers themselves in importance in the town. Mathias Read was invited by Elisha Gale in 1708 to undertake the altar piece and before 1713 he painted **The Last Supper**. This did a great deal to enhance his reputation as an artist. Some years after the altar piece had been placed in the chapel the same artist was employed to furnish it with two companions, and he accordingly painted two very good figures of Moses and Aaron each of them larger than life, which were placed on each side of the altar piece, under the galleries, to make the view from the principal entrance (by the west door) more complete. After the restoration of the church in 1883 these two paintings were moved to the west end and hung on either side of the entrance door. Miraculously they were thus saved when in 1971 a fire destroyed the organ loft and gutted most of the nave and all of the chancel. They now hang in St James Church. This church was enlarged by the addition of two wings in 1745-6.

Not only old churches were being rebuilt but as the century proceeded and the population continued to increase, entirely new ones were being built. One such was Holy Trinity Church built in 1715. From the "Holy Trinity Church Book, Accounts of Building of Church", in Whitehaven Library can be read:-

"Paid Mr Read in full for his part of the painting £9 in arrears collected from subscriptions £12.5.9¾ and in seats 18, 155, 213 £22.14.2¼ for his whole work he would have got in cash and in kind £44.7.1d".

Mr William Copeland an unknown artist was also paid for painting in the church, but Read was obviously painting the church fitments and an altar piece, **The Ascension.** This was destroyed by fire 31st August 1871 and all traces of his decorating would have disappeared. The church was modernized in 1886. It was finally demolished in 1947 and the Altar piece has gone. A long article in Whitehaven News 3rd February 1949 describes where all the fitments went.

Read's name is amongst the list of 125 subscribers towards this new church. On 1 February 1713 he gave the high sum of £10 which made him one of the chief benefactors. Only eleven, including Sir John Lowther, gave more.

Up until now no mention was made of Read's financial state and this is the first such mention. At least it confirms the remarks made by both Hutchinson and the Rev. Gilpin that Mathias Read became a popular and successful artist but it is worth noting that by this time Read had been in Whitehaven for twenty-three years.

The Church was dedicated to the Holy and undivided Trinity. Read also painted the Royal Arms. There is a reference in the Vestry Book to his being paid in 1718 for painting the King's Arms.[30]

Read's involvement with the Church included being "a vestry warden in 1715".[31] He also paid £12.0.0. for a pew – no.65 September 30th 1715. "This ticket entitles Mr Mathias Read His heirs exors admrs or asignes to the seat No 65 in the new church at Whitehaven according to the terms in the original subscription in consideration of 12 pounds by him actually paid

J Spedding
The Bell
Harry Walker
Thos Coates
Mick Threlkeld
(pencil) F Steele"[32]

The elegant St James Church was built 1752-53 in Whitehaven after Read's death so that it bears no direct relation to Read save for the fact that **Moses and Aaron** are now housed in the upper gallery.

After Sir John Lowther died in January 1706, his son James succeeded him and ceased spending so much time in Whitehaven. The evidence suggests he took much less notice of Read. His old friend William Gilpin was to die in 1724 and this seems to have been the end of the Gilpin family links. One new patron, Humphrey Senhouse, did employ him if briefly to paint a gilded monument for Crosscanonby Church (ill. 3) in 1727/8 to the memory of his two sons.[33]

There is still a faint trace of the gilding today on the tablet which is on the wall together with another probably decorated by Read. At the Senhouse Museum the Achievement of Arms of the Senhouse family is by Read.

At Penrith, the building of St Andrews Church was begun about 1718. Mathias Read was commissioned to do work for it including the Royal Arms dated 1723 which can still be seen. In 1722, when the Church was completed, he was invited to undertake the whole of the interior decoration – his estimate was accepted.[34] He also made the quotation for the altar-piece there and it reads "The Altar piece painted with any story

3 Senhouse Memorial (Crosscanonby)

shall be thought fitt not exceeding twenty figures – £20.0.0". Unfortunately, this painting was destroyed in 1845. A contemporary description by Walker[35] of it is of interest: "shortly after the church was rebuilt, the task of adorning the chancel, which is enclosed in a semi-circular recess, was entrusted to a painter named Reed. On the south wall of the chancel, this artist executed in oil colour a life-size figure of the patron Saint with his cross; on the north, a group representing one of our Saviour's miracles;

whilst the upper portion of the arch was filled with a choir of angels playing on musical instruments, amongst which might be recognised a modern organ and a bass viol." Walker goes on to say "From the effects of damp and neglect these pictures were nearly obliterated; even the lime plaster on which they had been painted was beginning to decay, when, at a vestry meeting held in the year 1845, it was resolved that the chancel should be repaired."

Hutchinson[36] also noted the altar which he considered "well illuminated, and adorned with suitable paintings, in a tolerable style; the choral bands in the clouds, being encumbered with a large bass-viol, is an absurdity derived from the work of a great master, which he copied, but would have been better had he corrected it".

Bass-viol or not, no trace of this altar-piece or this decoration remains upon which to comment today. However it may be of interest to print his Accounts for the work.[37] So at the vestry meeting in 1845 it was agreed to adorn the chancel with new paintings and interestingly enough the work was entrusted to one of the Lake District's greatest nineteenth Century painters Jacob Thompson of Penrith.[38]

Read's patrons included Matthias Gale, his neighbour in Cross Street.

In the will of this merchant and neighbour dated 1751 it is recorded that Gale made bequests to his sons John and Robert which included work by Read.

1751 "Matthias Gale, merchant . . . to my son John . . . my now dwelling house with the statues, potts and other appurtenances of the garden and my own and his mother's picture done by Mr Hide with a picture of King Charles 1, also the Christian Triumph, the battlepiece between Alexander and Darien with various tents, Achilles, Anger and Whitehaven with their framing and appurtenances . . . also mine and my father's picture in miniature . . ."

". . . to my son Robert Gale the picture of Susannah and the Elders and the three ships; also the picture of myself, his mother and grandmother with that of his Uncle Robert Ponsonby done by Mr Read with his own picture done by Mr Wolston and all their frames and appurtenances with my daughter Mary's harpsichord all my music books and papers."

Nothing would have been known about Read's health had not Dr Brownrigg, his doctor, left immaculate notes on his patients. It may be of interest to print an extract from these covering his final ten years.

Dr Brownrigg's Medical Report on Mr Read

"Mr Rhead the famous artist

1738 January

A man of about seventy. Very thin and of a melancholy disposition living a very temperate way of life, of a peevish nature and utterly wrapped up in his work. For most of his life he had had no illnesses with the exception of gout, but his attacks of this disease had been only slight, and rarely causing any systemic upset.

However being intolerant of pain, five years ago he wanted to avoid this problem by taking cold baths: as a result his pain promptly came back . . ."

There follows an itemized account of the pain and discomfort of his illness which lasted on and off from 13th January to 28th March. His attempts to cure himself with cold baths on 13th January resulted in the pains recurring with increased violence. To quote Dr Brownrigg the pains "assailed the wretched man", and it seemed that he was indeed suffering greatly and not able to endure it. "He was moaning and groaning continually" "But as was his habit he remained in very low spirits throughout the attack".[39,40]

On November 8th 1747 Read died aged 78 and was buried in Holy Trinity churchyard. After a thorough search of the little garden now known as Trinity Gardens, where the gravestones from Holy Trinity Church are housed there appears no sign of Mathias' tombstone. Daniel Hay described its siting some years ago and said it was much worn.

The Whitehaven Herald for 2nd May 1874 mentions his tombstone. Joseph Wear, the reporter, writes:

"Here lies interr'd the Body of M(r) Mathias Read, Painter, who died November the 8 1747, Aged 78 years. Here also lies Mrs Elizabeth Read, his wife, who died April ye 12th, 1748 in ye 79th year of her Age . . .

In giving the above few particulars of an almost forgotten celebrity, we cannot but express a hope that the authorities of Trinity Church will not grudge what little labour or even expense may be necessary in keeping the headstone of the Read family in a condition which will ensure the memory of the painter of the principal altar pieces in the town being kept green amongst us for a generation or two to come."

From the deeds of the house on Cross Street, it is understood that it was to pass according to Mathias's will to his wife, then to her sister Mary and her eldest daughter. The Gibsons and their family held the house until

1809. According to the census of 1762, from 1756-1772 Joseph and Henry Hinde, both painters, lived in it, and also William Palmer, a carpenter.

Read's artistic interests were continued by his nephew Joseph Hinde who is known to have copied some of the paintings in the Hall. When Sir James died in 1755 it was Joseph who arranged for the despatch of his entire collection of 144 paintings from Flatt Hall to Holker, and he wrote the long list of them and even painted pictures in it.[41] They went naturally enough for those days, by sea. One other member of the Hinde family, Joseph's brother Henry, was also a painter. These two are important in that they make a link between Read and later Whitehaven painters, notably Strickland Lowry.

There used to be several headstones marking the burials of further members of the Hinde family, but now few remain.

1 View of Whitehaven from the sea by Jan Wyck

2 Naworth Castle

3 Isel Hall from the North

4 Isel Hall from the South

5 A Landscape with a Cumbrian Village and Church

6 Calder Abbey

7 View of Lowther

8 Ouse Bridge

9 Carlisle from Stanwix

10 Pool on the River Eden

11 View of Whitehaven

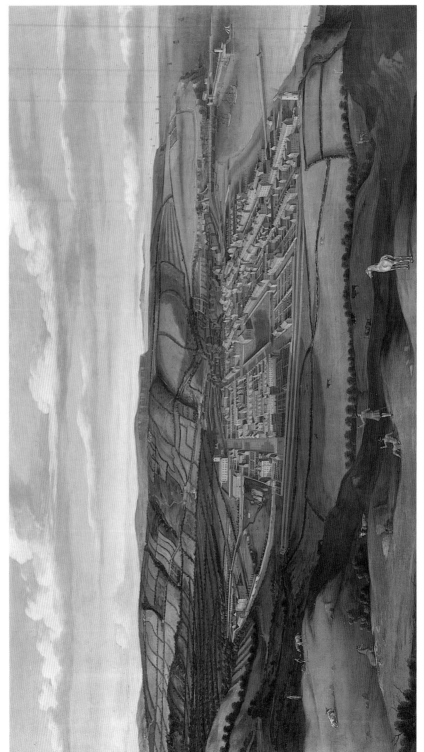

12 A Prospect of Whitehaven from Brackenthwaite

13 A Prospect of Whitehaven

14 A bird's Eye View of Whitehaven

15 View of Whitehaven Port

16 View of Parton

CHAPTER 3

LANDSCAPE THROUGH READ'S EYE

At first glance, the aerial format of much of Read's work may seem unexpected to today's audience. It should not. Nearly four thousand years ago extant plans of Egyptian gardens were drawn from above with each object shown in elevation. Early Chinese and later Persian and Indian artists used this method for both landscape (often battle scenes) and domestic subjects. There is evidence of the pre-Columbian Incas using the same technique. Certainly in Hellenistic and Roman painting the aerial perspective was a well-accepted device e.g. the Vatican's Odysseus frescoes; the Pompeian landscape frescoes and some Attic fragments. It seems therefore a fairly universal method of presenting to the viewer a topic in a succinct and mildly dramatic way. There are advantages in showing the separateness of each subject, and it gives scope for design in the relationships of these subjects. Perhaps, most importantly, it solves some of the problems of displaying the middle ground. Today's man is much more conversant with this technique than he may suppose. Most television sporting events are broadcast in this way. Both films and TV use the method extensively to show more clearly what is happening during interior scenes (drama and current affairs), and in exterior action sequences. The structure of theatres themselves creates an aerial view for the majority of the audience; consider the placing of royal boxes. In recent years it has not been uncommon to see operatic and theatrical productions deliberately use a stage that slopes quite steeply up to the backdrop, partially to enhance the dramatic effect. It is interesting that the ancient White Horse of Uffington was made on the brow of a down, so making it almost impossible to see properly from other than a bird's eye view, although how such a position was achieved is not easy to speculate.

When showing a Read to a museum friend, he said "Ah, a primitive." Perhaps it is wrong to think that this was meant as a slightly deprecatory statement, and certainly most people would think of Read in this "primitive" category. The O.E.D. defines primitive as "having the quality of that which is early or ancient; simple, rude, rough". One reason for the primitive label in Read's case is his use of the bird's eye technique which has been shown to have a long and honourable history. Yet, there is a feeling in the word primitive that man's potential as an artist has yet to be developed, just as cave art may still be thought primitive. E. H. Gombrich[42] suggests that cave art as we can see it today may be anything but primitive in that it may well be an art form which has evolved to the needs of that society over thousands of years.

In these bird's eye landscapes there is a sense of detachment and natural tranquillity which is often lost in the romantic and picturesque, when "Nature" was elevated to an academic cult. With a few exceptions, notably Samuel Palmer, this peacefulness had gone by the nineteenth century. This aura of quiet permanence may well have appealed to the inner needs of the gentry for whom the Civil War, the Restoration, and Dutch William's enthronement were the recent past. Somehow the figures, human and animal, mostly seem to be looking serenely into the picture in the same direction as the viewer and even when portrayed in movement do not disturb the peace of the scene. Today one hears endless moans about the deterioration of the English landscape due to modern farming methods. Man thinks he likes the ease of a constant environment. Read's gentry were living through the great agricultural revolution and may have felt the same way about the countryside they knew and loved. The pictograms of the Egyptian tombs of seasons and agricultural scenes were to give the dead soul a sense of continuity and eternity. It is suggested that this bird's eye genre of landscape painting may have done the same for the living.

During the pre-renaissance in Italy increasing interest was paid to the rocky gothic backgrounds of the religious subjects and perhaps Mantegna was one who was instrumental in organising these visual accessories into a formalised landscape. He was concerned with the geology and true structure of his surroundings. It was his brother in law, Giovanni Bellini who painted the most exquisite natural landscapes of the renaissance and solved the essential problem of penetration into the distance. He manages with spatial geometry to interrelate the parallel planes of the middle distance and to combine it with a marvellous understanding of the quality of light in the countryside. It is thought that this appreciation of light was enhanced by the influence of the Flemish artists such as Jan van Eyck. Most painters at this time continued to utilise a raised view point. Van Eyck solved the recession of the middle distance by using meandering rivers, trees, buildings and interrelated groups of active men and animals. Were it not for the renaissance obsession for man and his works, it might be surprising that the great Tuscan painters of the Quattrocento, with the possible exception of Pierro della Francesca, Antonio Pollaiolo and Fra Bartolomeo, took so little interest in their countryside. The fascinating Tuscan landscape with its hills and hilltop villages, the escarpments and rivers, the forests and cultivation, naturally solves all the landscape painters' technical problems.

The middle distance does not seem to have caused much trouble to great painters, but it gave rise to many difficulties for lesser men amongst whom was Read. The mantle of natural landscape painting, as opposed to idealised or fantastic landscape, passed via Bosch and Breughel to the Dutch painters of the seventeenth century. In the National Gallery there is a remarkable landscape (mid fifteenth century) behind Dieric Bouts' "Entombment"; almost monochromatic and devoid of any obvious stratagem, he shows a beautiful softly receding winter countryside.

Holland by this time was a very rich bourgeois country. The citizens liked having themselves and their property portrayed, and they liked landscapes of the country they knew. With the flatness of the countryside it must have been a great help to many to use the aerial perspective. Although Rembrandt in his simplest of sketches, with a view point below the elbow height of a foreground observer, shows how a flat countryside poses no problem to genius.

There has always been a close relationship, albeit sometimes competitive, between the Netherlands and Britain. This was strengthened after the Restoration when Royal patronage brought the Van der Veldes to London and again enhanced by William III. David Solkin in his catalogue for his great Richard Wilson exhibition suggests, in Britain, the leisured patricians preferred the "Italian" arcadian ideal of the idle shepherd in the happy rural life. While the more industrious landowners of the seventeenth and eighteenth centuries were more concerned with practical agricultural husbandry to improve their estates and other assets. These men, of intelligent bourgeois habits, preferred the bourgeois Netherlandish realism. Possibly in this association with their land, they became aware of the harmony of which man is capable with his environment, so sowing the seed of interest in landscape, and opening a new avenue of painting expression which had been dominated by portraiture during the reign of Queen Elizabeth. The artist turned his eyes from the captive model, the king in his castle; from the inside looking out, to looking at the castle from outside. From painting pictures of static dead fowl and pheasants, bowls of fruit and flowers, he looked at real nature, the live landscape, at the outside world and how man and his castle fitted into it. He even showed the landowner walking about his estate and looking at his house and property, often accompanied by and talking to his henchmen. However, both patricians and the bourgeois intelligentsia made use of the Dutch aerial manner. It became a very British art form of which Mathias Read was one of the very few early, English exponents.

Topographical pictures are more common in Britain than on the continent – although in the latter, such great palaces as Versailles became common in painting especially after 1800. In Britain all manner of scenes were done as early as 1650 and in some cases even earlier. In 1642 Wencelas Hollar drew Albury Place, Surrey. It was his later work which helped to make topographical book illustrations popular. There followed Dugdale's "Monasticum Anglicanum" (1655-73) and "The Antiquities of Warwickshire Illustrated" (1656). Perhaps the drawing by John Evelyn of Wotton House, Surrey, in 1653 is the earliest example of recording a country house and garden in Britain.[43]

There were a number of influential topographical artists, such as Hendrick Danckerts, Thomas Wyck, Jacob Knyff and Johananes Vostermann. Perhaps of those who contributed most to this new art was Jan Siberechts who came to London in 1673. By 1726 came the countrywide study of monastic architecture in Nathaniel Buck's "Antiquities". Indeed it was partly due to the backing of the Society of Antiquaries, whose first secretary, William Stukeley, was appointed in 1717, that the great fashion for publishing topographical views flourished and made Britain foremost in this field.

In 1707 engravings after Leonard Knyff's prospects of great houses was published. Behind these and other views of great properties lay the pride of the owners. They wished to show their estates in as full a way as possible and record in every detail the buildings and the improvements they had carried out. The greatest attention was paid to even the smallest item.

Peter Tillemans (c.1684-1734), born in Antwerp, was a popular topographical artist. He had been trained by Teniers and also did battle pictures. He came to England in 1708 and created a strong interest by his drawings of topographical views of Oxford and Northamptonshire, prospects of Newmarket and views of country houses. There is a resemblance of style between Tillemans and Read. In the Lowther Collection there were two pictures by Tillemans, **A view of Furness Abbey in water colour** and **Horse and Groom**. Could Read have met him?[44]

Sir Kenneth Clark[45] writes of the eighteenth century as being the winter of the imagination when the landscape of fact degenerates to topography and the landscape of fantasy to the picturesque. Is this school of house portraiture just topography? Surely Siberechts painting of **Ham House from Richmond Hill** and his **Bifrons in Kent** and Danckerts' **Troy House**

near Monmouth are not simply topography. Although all three are seventeenth century, what sets such as these apart from other well known names and pictures is their splendid inclusion of the surrounding countryside, and the *Englishness* of its handling.

Following in Jan Wyck's shoes, Read painted for his benefactor and patron, Sir John Lowther, in the Netherlandish manner, the townscapes and house portraits that were required. Perhaps the aerial technique is not as well suited to portraying a mountainous landscape (which it diminishes) as the flat lands of Holland. Although Stephen Penn in his drawings of Thurston Water introduces a charming drama with his portrayal of the surrounding mountains. It was however the expected and well accepted method of the day. But by the beginning of the eighteenth century, it was a convention in danger of becoming conventional and hence becoming unworthy of attention. Of course some patrons will have insisted on their estates being portrayed in the accepted manner. It is possible to see in Read's work, the beginnings of the transformation from a purely topographical house portrait to a landscape painting in which there is a recognisable building, as can be seen in the Ouse Bridge, Haile, and Isel group. In his later landscapes the influence of the seventeenth century Roman School, perhaps for the first time in English art, begins to make its appearance. Because of the difficulty in dating many of the pictures, a purely chronological change cannot be described.

The recent exhibition of English water-colours at the Royal Academy was an excellent opportunity to ponder the transition from topography to a landscape which imposes a serious personal psychological experience on the viewer. Each observer may draw his or her own boundaries between the two but it may still be possible to define some common ground to make such assessments. Colour, for instance, ceases to be just decorative and is used to produce an ambience. This psychological sensation will be enhanced with the use of a wide variety of apparent textures of the work's components, which are seldom seen in topography. The painter's view point can be chosen to create in the subject a juxtaposition of planes and solid shapes, and build an interest not dissimilar to a still-life; likewise groups of animals, human or others, may be used to the same effect. In topographical work the use of light is largely chiaroscuro whilst the successful landscape artist uses light with all its atmospheric manifestations. Again the truly gifted painter was able to fill the work with all sorts of accurate detail, which whilst there for all to see, seems to fade to insignificance because of the power of the picture to concentrate and hold the beholder's mind on the artist's vision. It is not claimed that Read fulfilled all these criteria but he seems consciously aware of moving away from the old topographical conventions.

On some occasions Read was presumably able to persuade the various patrons of his house portraits that the house might be painted very small so as to include as much as possible of their estate. This seems to have given him the opportunity to move towards a less rigid style. As he remained popular and in demand it may be assumed that the landowners liked the result. (How interesting it would be to know if they liked the painting because the land was theirs or because they thought it beautiful.) He would have had to paint the surrounding countryside in a recognisable and correct topographical manner. Although he could choose his view- point, he was obliged to paint the fells and fields as they were. There would be no opportunity to select various geographic subjects to make up his picture. This helps to increase the naivety of his paintings but also gives them a fresh veracity. Indeed Ruskin states "go to nature . . . selecting nothing, rejecting nothing, scorning nothing . . ."[46] The paintings of Isel and Haile Hall are good examples. He so cleverly composed the views that he must have done a large amount of drawing from nature. He combines all the broad salient features into the composition and yet had an eye for the many important details. Yet all this is done from a view point above any available high point of land. In both Isel views, the house has been reduced to a small but accurate vignette and we see a marvellously sensual fellscape quite unlike the known Dutch masters of the genre. As the river Derwent is not visible, these two views are rare examples of good landscape without any water, which is uncommon.

In Read's painting we can see the enduring sensual strength and simplicity of the Cumbrian mountains which have sustained the admiration and love of so many generations, and which re-emerge with Sheila Fell in this century. Read was not just the "Father" of Cumbrian painting but remains one of the very few who, to this day, have been able to do due justice to these mountains and fells.

Particularly, but not only, in the Isel pictures he has painted the most remarkable skies and for Constable "the sky was the chief organ of sentiment". There are strong similarities with those painted in Venice in the sixteenth century. Here are the streaming cumulus clouds on a blue background and edged with pinks and deep yellow-gold that can be seen so often on the Cumbrian western horizon in the summer and autumn. It would be fascinating to know if, and how, he had ever seen a Giorgione or

Titian sky . Perhaps the skies are an amalgam of nicely observed fact and of original thought. He painted forcefully and accurately what he saw. They are wonderful skies. There were not many English painters until Constable who gave such importance to this subject. Below these skies the distant mountain tops are alive with light and shade to reveal their character.

However, his awareness of the effect of the moist atmosphere on this mountain light is most unusual at this date in Britain, and his technique and ability in painting these opacities is remarkable. The painting of distant mountains in this way would surely not have come from his Dutch confrères and there is even less chance he could have learned this from a British source. However Read had his shortcomings. Principally he never managed to overcome satisfactorily the problem of the distance receding in his middle ground. He tried to achieve a sense of depth by painting men and animals of decreasing size the further they were from his view point. Here one may recall Samuel Palmer's words "Landscape is of little value, but as it hints or expresses the haunts and doings of man. However gorgeous, it can be but paradise without an Adam". We know from his portraits and the animals in the **Last Boar Hunt** that he was a competent figure technician. Usually however the figures in his landscapes are weakly constructed and quickly done, although with some humour. He will often have a group of onlookers who may be talking and gesticulating or just lying about in a languid fashion in the foreground. The gentrified folk in the Lowther picture contrast sharply with the lively group of carousing locals in Tullie House's **View of Whitehaven**. He sometimes will have a horse or two also looking onto the scene. It is much easier to paint horses from the back! They look into the picture as if to stimulate the curiosity of the viewer, in the same way that it is difficult not to be curious about what a street crowd has gathered for. Could they be a residuum of donors looking to the scene of some religious topic which they have funded? In so placing these foreground figures, he sets up the size guide for those men and animals which act as scale sign posts in the middle distance. It is perhaps interesting to note that when the late Innocenti was asked to design small if grandiose gardens, he placed the smaller trees and shrubs in the distance, graduating to the large ones close-by, giving an extraordinary sense of depth to a small garden. In the final airport scene of the film "Casablanca", the planes were cardboard cut-outs and the humans were dwarfs on a small set to give a surprising illusion of depth and distance. Sometimes, however, Read tends to forget to relate the size of these figures with other lateral objects in the picture. This suggests that they may have been added as an afterthought to try to increase the sense of depth, particularly as the paint is thin in some cases. All these figures, men and animals, are also used to add to the animation of the canvasses. His interest in the animals is evident, e.g. the way he shows a dog as if it were conversing with a horse **(Isel from the North)**. This can result sometimes in the intimate details of the picture becoming more engrossing than the whole. The dog racing between the two groups of people in **Carlisle from Stanwix** adds an air of interest to the picture. Also the speed of the dog and the free handling of the paint in this picture, as in the **Naworth Castle,** show a style quite in advance of his times. His depiction of horse movement was less convincing.

To return to the middle distance problems, he uses a road with travellers receding to the distance in **Carlisle from Stanwix** and the unrecognised **Cumbrian church and village with mountains**. This is not very successful partially because the roads are very dull. Sadly he does not seem to have been able to use some of the sinuous Cumbrian rivers which might have served him rather better. Although he used the atmospheric opacity in a masterly way for the far distances there is no sign of his trying to introduce this method of depth gradation for the middle ground, already an established manoeuvre in the Pompeian frescoes and presumably other classical works. Maybe his sponsors did not want a hazy Hall.

As with most of his rural pictures there is a predominance of green in his palette and this seems over the years to have become too blue in patches. Perhaps it was not easy to obtain the best of pigments in Whitehaven.

In his canvasses of Whitehaven this problem of middle distance is more or less resolved by the nature of the new town. The geometric planning was ideally suited to a renaissance perspective treatment and this, if a little stark, admirably overcomes these difficulties. He must have been standing on what is called now Sunny Hill. Unfortunately later building prevents us from seeing the same view today, but it gave him a good point of departure for these splendid bird's eye views. In Abbot Hall's **Calder Abbey** he fills the whole of the middle ground with the Abbey itself. The foreground and sides are all dark and contrast dramatically with the bright pale stone work of the buildings. This is a great dramatic success. Although the layout is paralleled in other artists' work at this time, his use of light in this way seems to be his own. Little of the park is visible and this would not have suited some of his patrons, but the hills behind are properly displayed.

We know from Hinde's list of paintings, transferred from Flatt Hall to Holker about 1756, that there were about thirty undated, unspecified landscapes whose authorship is not recorded. However one is labelled **"66. Copy of an Italian Landscape by Read after – . . . No.12"**. It would not be unreasonable to suppose that at least a few others were of Italian origin (another is described "a prospect . . . in the Mediterranean"). This could have been one demonstrable source of the increasing Italian influence on Read's composition which is specifically referred to in the following commentaries on each individual picture. It is of considerable interest that while using these Italianesque compositional structures, his landscapes appear neither Italian nor Netherlandish, but completely English and especially Cumbrian. His better work predates that of Wootton, Lambert and Wilson by 20 years or more. This is not to compare Read with Wilson, but perhaps Ruskin's belief that with Wilson "sincere landscape art . . . begins in England", might have been tempered by travelling to see the Reads in his neighbours' houses in Cumbria.

Read also made presentable portraits and his religious works were highly thought of in his lifetime but their remains are now difficult to assess. He seems to have been the first natural landscape painter of Cumbria, and perhaps, with the noble exception of Blacklock, until this century, the only one. It is ironic that his pupil's grandson should have been a prime mover of the rigid picturesque movement which held the lake district painting in bondage for nearly two hundred years. Sadly few of his paintings remain but all the more reason that they should be more widely known and admired. It is good to see Cumbrian buildings as they were two hundred and fifty or more years ago, but his ability to paint the Cumbrian skies, peaks and air, and especially the strong undulating mountain country was powerful and unique. In an increasingly transitory world his work is a great comfort. Mathias Read blows down the centuries like a fresh mountain breeze on a summer's day.

4 Italianate Landscape (Holker Hall)

VIEW OF WHITEHAVEN FROM THE SEA.   Lord Cavendish of Furness,
                                            Holker Hall, Cumbria.

(Jan Wyck). (1640-1702) Signed and dated, lower right, 1686.

Oil on canvas   15" x 44¾" (38.1 x 113.6 cms)

A distinguished painting showing the town in the late seventeenth century before all the developments took place. The dark turgid water and subdued greens are perhaps indications of Wyck's influence on Read. The beautiful precision and clarity in the separate delineation of each stone making up the quay wall, is also a pointer to Read's later depiction of buildings. The lovely little brightly coloured details of figures with their specks of red and of seagulls, flags and pennants on masts give visual light and relief to the painting. To the right, the cliffs, where later were situated the "Hurries", show an interesting sight of what it once looked like.

The town houses are all painted in very pale tones of light beige. They are neither obviously of pink sandstone nor of greenstone but could represent rendered surfaces.

Colour plate 1.

At Malahide Castle, on loan from the National Gallery of Dublin, is Jan Wyck's vast painting of the **Battle of the Boyne** (219 x 302cms). It is signed by J. Wyck and dated 1693 and depicts the battle of 1st July 1690, between William III and the exiled pretender James. James had come to Ireland for the support he was unable to gather in England and Scotland.

A great sweeping landscape sets the battle scene, where the armies are seen massed in the middle distance with the two leaders clearly shown in the foreground. Their armour, horse regalia and costume are picked out with highlights. It is this landscape which is so striking in relation to Read's painting. Two similarities in style are immediately apparent; the high puffy white and pink cumulus clouds soaring above the hills, and the rather blue-green colour of the paint in the grass fields. In both these can be seen the influence of Wyck on his pupil. Could Read possibly have had a hand in painting the background?

27

5 Widewath

WIDEWATH.   Private Collection.

Landscape with a small white farm

Oil on panel c.1700

Provenance: Lot 56. Sothebys 21st November 1979

Widewath is in Heltondale, near Askham, one mile south west of Helton. The manor of Helton was sold to Sir John Lowther in 1680, so this painting would have been done for him by Read. The mill is still there but disused, but there is no trace of the mill pond. Trees have grown up to interrupt the view of Widewath itself but it is recognisable. The initials R. M. I. and date 1676 appear over the doorway.

There is a reference to Widewath in Nicholson & Burn who transcribe a document of early 15th Century date, and this is recorded in the C & W of 1921.

> "Item Stokthawyte and Wythwathe. Item ij
> acrs off lond in Whale yt lyeth by the the [bek] e"[47]

This most linear landscape appears to be very early. It shows a small white rather 'self conscious' farm surrounded by neat walls, young trees, and a few animals all conforming to a strict perspective. There are some curious features in the painting. A river flowing from left to right across the painting provides a water supply for a mill in the lower right and below this some curiously painted boulders convey the idea of stepping-stones from this side of the stream, which flows from the river, to the mill building. Wath is a lake district name for a ford or crossing.

The dogs in the picture are Rache, a large slow hound brought to England by the Normans. During the reign of James I in 1613 they were spelt alternatively as Brache. But before and after that date were commonly known by the name Rache. They had generally disappeared by 1830 but lingered in the Borders where they had been used continuously to control and hunt out reivers so they were really man hunters.

The animals and figures are rather wooden so that at first sight it looks even too stiff to have been painted by Read, but on examining the rider on horseback in the lower left hand of the panel, it is unmistakably his style. Another figure, a servant, is striding up the hill towards him. He is curiously painted with arms folded and wearing a wide brimmed hat, no doubt of felt. It all looks like a toy landscape where someone has dropped the figures and animals down at random.

Illustration 5.

6 Blencowe Hall detail, cattle

7 Blencowe Hall

BLENCOWE HALL, CUMBRIA.

Keith Darby, Esq.,
Warnell Hall, Sebergham.

Oil on canvas c.1700   27¹/₂" x 35¹/₄" (69.2 x 89.2 cms)

"William de Greystoke served with the Black Prince in invasion into France and one of his followers was Adam de Blencowe. He and his successors enjoyed privileges and considerations from the Lord of Greystoke in whose Barony, Blencow was situated, It was much battered by cannon shells in the civil wars and never fully restored"

"The remains of a small chapel still exist, situated in the west side of the courtyard, a portion of the east window has been preserved in the gable and facing the quadrangle; it consists of an acutely pointed arch, recessed with round and hollow mouldings, divided by a chamfered shaft into the pointed lights, without cusps or tracing".[48]

The picture was painted for the Blencowe family of Blencowe Hall, whence by inheritance to their kinsman Sir John Blencowe (1642-1746) Judge of Marston St Lawrence, Oxfordshire, and then by linear descent until 1988 in that house. The family is now extinct. The family had held Marston from Tudor times until the mid 1930s. The other branch of the family who lived at Blencowe subsequently lived at Thoby Priory, Essex.

It is a gentle picture of an almost almond colour with greys and greens. The back of the house is shown as if it were then the front. At the sale of this picture in 1988 a Victorian photograph of Blencowe was sold also; it was taken from the other side which had by that time been regarded as the front.

The stream flowing on the right fills three rectangular ponds edged with stone. These were possibly fish-ponds. Three ducks float on the foremost and two long-horned cows and a horse are grazing in the field by the ponds. A spaniel-like dog races towards a horsedrawn vehicle entering in the far right. This is black with high red wheels, perhaps a phaeton.

In the centre left a man in a tricorne hat is standing in front of the cross on the wall of the ruined chapel. The lower foreground shows ploughed soil. The appearance of the house suggests the surfaces were then rendered. The picture primarily concentrates on the house and little attention is paid to the sky, composition or human content. It was probably an early commercial house painting.

Illustrations 6 & 7.

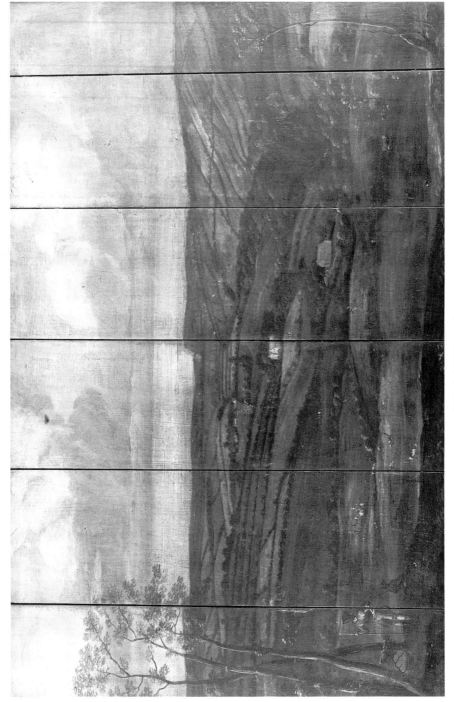

8 Haile Hall from the east

HAILE HALL FROM THE EAST.   Private Collection.

Oil on panel (6 boards) c.1710   30¾" x 46¼" (78.1 x 117.4 cms)

Haile has been the home of the same family since mediaeval times, the picture has never been moved since Mathias Read painted it. The view is of the house in the middle distance with the sea behind, with the sloping cliff known as Warbra Nook on the horizon. It was painted from the valley rising behind the house to the east. There is a barn which no longer exists in the foreground. The rest of the landscape is rural and divided into many fields.

In the lower left two figures survey the scene, and a pair of huntsmen are mounted and being watched by a cow. There are several hounds in the fields.

The house is depicted with two wings. It is one of his very green pictures and is dappled with light with one of his typical wind-swept skies, cumulus cloud against blue. It is interesting to see how he has begun to frame his pictures with spindly trees.

In his lovely composition he has manipulated the natural pattern made by the fields, hedges and trees to focus on the house, nestling in the centre of the picture. The figure represented helps to strengthen this attention.

Illustration 8.

9 Haile Hall (south) detail, greyhound and huntsman

10 Haile Hall (south) detail, house

HAILE HALL from the south.   Private Collection.

Oil on panel c.1710   36³/₄" x 47¹/₄" (94¹/₂ x 122.3 cms)

This view is taken from the south towards the Gatehouse, not visible in the previous picture. The house is shown in the middle distance; and two men with staves stand with two seated hounds in the lower right in the shade of a tree. The landscape is predominantly fields but trees line the river bed and a road runs away from the gatehouse. One of these trees is still there today. Horned cattle graze in the middle distance. Although the house is more clearly defined, this composition is not so impressive as the previous one.

Illustrations 9, 10 & 11.

11 Haile Hall from the South

12 Naworth Castle detail, dovecot

13 Naworth Castle detail, stag

14 Naworth Castle detail, horse and hounds

36

NAWORTH CASTLE.

The Hon. Philip Howard,
Naworth Castle, Cumbria.

Oil on canvas c.1715 $33^{1}/_{4}$" x $54^{1}/_{4}$" (84.4 x 137.7 cms)

Naworth Castle is shown with very warm glowing light on its red sandstone walls. The peach coloured clouds and the sunlight on the castle show his favourite evening light. In his application of the paint he has used a rather smooth and sometimes even smudgy effect similar to that in **Carlisle from Stanwix** and Tullie House's **View of Whitehaven**. This technique denies us a detailed understanding of the stonework.

The dovecot on the right of the picture is rather badly drawn and appears to have been added as the indication of earlier paint can be seen through it. However it forms an important part of the composition. The shape of the castle dictates the dimensions of the picture and to some extent the surrounding landscape. No other picture by Read handles the trees on the left side so elegantly, in some ways reminiscent of early seventeenth century French landscape. He has most skilfully managed the fences, lines of hounds and walls in the foreground to converge on the castle. Behind this there is a backdrop of the Cumbrian mountains and a pleasantly hedged fellside which again leads in towards the building.

Both men and animals show a diversity of treatment. Whilst the hounds are well portrayed, the stag they pursue is rather skittish, as is the 'Chiricoesque' horse watching them. On the other hand the three hunt servants and their horses are well drawn with attention paid to their faces. There is a nervous young person watching the hunt from an old turret in the castle wall. This portrayal of rustic life gives an air of animation and jollity to the scene. Although the structure and execution of this picture is dissimilar to most of his other work, it stands out as one of the most important.

Cover & colour plate 2. Illustrations 12, 13 & 14.

15 Isel Hall (north) detail, mower

16 Isel Hall (north) detail, house

ISEL HALL FROM THE NORTH. Private Collection.

Oil on canvas 1710-1718   39" x 50$\frac{1}{2}$" (98.8 x 127.1 cms)

One of a pair of Read's striking paintings, this is taken from the Clints, a high vantage point just to the North of Isel. Behind are the varying contours of Setmurthy forest and the Whiteside and Grassmoor ranges. What is now heavy forestry plantation was then fields surrounded by hedges. Despite the distance from Isel and the artist's viewpoint, Read has shown amazing detail. In examining the house through a magnifying glass, the lines of the roof tiles are indicated but the walls are smooth, being almost certainly rendered at that period. A double line of trees encloses the house and Pele Tower. The entrance is shown directly opposite the sunken garden which it used to cross. The Hall itself reveals a surprising wing of which this is the only accurate record. Its remains are illustrated in a drawing of about 80 years later. But in this view it ends in a tower, possibly a dovecot, or banqueting hall which were fashionable in the mid seventeenth century. This wing projects from the Northern face across the courtyard. A little building does stand out near where Isel Cottage is now, and whose ground plan is still extant today. The river is hidden behind wooded banks. Isel Bridge is shown humped as it was originally. Isel church is shown with a spire as is a church in one of the pictures of Whitehaven where no spire was previously known. There is, however, evidence on the ground at Isel Church of there once being a tower.

The picture is flanked on the right with a 'compositional' tree under which lounges, in typical exaggerated pose, a freely but well painted worker his scythe blade pointing over his shoulder. A mounted horseman in a wide brimmed black felt hat comes up towards the reclining workman. Details of a horse and dog playing and tiny figures of cattle and horses appear in the eliptical near foreground.

To the right a fairly large complex must indicate Hewthwaite Hall built two centuries before. Watch Hill and the Hay lie behind. Away in the far distance on the left is a little of the shore line of Bassenthwaite showing a building which is the Scarness Dower House, where his work was commissioned later.

This exceptional composition has been constructed by again using the many natural lines of topographical structure allied with a most skilful use of light on the fields to focus attention on the exquisite miniature house portrait.

Painted in morning sunshine every detail of the house is clearly defined. This same light delineates the tops of the mountains in a pioneering way for the date. Under the imposing sky he manipulates the light to unite an extensive and varied landscape.

Colour plate 3. Illustrations 15, 16, 17, 18 & 19.

17 Isel Hall (north) detail, Isel church

18 Isel Hall (north) detail, Isel bridge

19   Isel Hall (north) detail, horse and dog

40

ISEL HALL FROM THE SOUTH.   Private Collection.

Oil on canvas 1715-1718   38¼" x 49" (97.1 x 124.4 cms)

The second of the pair is painted from the southern side of the river beside Setmurthy forest and again provides a great deal of interesting information. What is now a forest appears to be mostly arable land interspersed with rows of trees, hedges and a few stone walls. The Clints, a limestone paved area, shows above the trees, and is still only sparsely covered. On the left the little village of Blindcrake appears to have more houses than at present. One tiny farmstead stands near the top of the hill, Thackray a house demolished by vandals in the last few decades. The field boundaries both below and above Isel Hall converge towards it, above the Hall the straight prominent walls were the ten foot stone deer park boundaries. Now most of the land is heavily wooded. Again the river is hidden between high banks, except for a small stretch. To-day from the same vantage point it is impossible to see it. The Hall and its stable yard building both appear but not the Grange as this was built later in the century.

Two pairs of men talk in the lower left corner – the two on the extreme left are lolling on the rocks, and the two in blue and brown coats possibly the owner (Sir Wilfrid Lawson 3rd Bart.) and a friend. One in each group is gesticulating as he talks. The insertion of cows of various sizes is meant to help to give a feeling of depth in the centre and further down the slope. The deciduous trees are often outlined by those characteristically 'snow like' highlights sometimes in the shape of flying birds, which led the owner of one painting to think the men standing by the tree in question were training 'hawks' but they were really highlights in the bushes!

With masterly handling of the morning light Read has created one of his best skies. He uses the light to reveal the detail of the small escarpments in the otherwise dark foreground. This in itself anticipates the standardized late Georgian English landscape 'framing'. He even uses the centrally placed rectangular area enclosed by trees as a stage on which to feature the house.

Colour plate 4.

A LANDSCAPE WITH A CUMBRIAN VILLAGE
AND CHURCH.

Private Collection.

Oil on Canvas c.1718   36" x 41" (92 x 104 cms)

Provenance: Lord Brougham. This painting was offered for sale at Sothebys on 11th July 1984, Lot 83.

In the foreground is the boundary of a park, over the wall a yokel peers inquisitively inwards.

There are two men talking with a horse and a foal to their right. A cow browses just below them and there are other animals scattered about. A sweeping curve of little bushes runs from the trees to the right into the picture taking the eye to a Church on a little hillock near the horizon. Dappled light in the foreground contrasts with areas shaded by clouds and the whole picture appears lighter and calmer than some of Read's work. This is enhanced by the beauty of the sky. It is unusual in having a well-lit bright proscenium which helps to set up the taut design of the main features of the picture. Altogether the soft colouring creates a mood of a warm summer evening, in a gentle rustic setting.

At the time of Sotheby's sale the attribution of 'A View of the Langdales from South of Kendal, with Crinkle Crags, Bowfell and Coniston Old Man', seemed to fit but on having seen the picture itself in 1992, it is clearly not a view of the Langdales from the South of Kendal. No alternative site has been established to date.

Colour plate 5.

43

CALDER ABBEY.   Abbot Hall Art Gallery, Kendal.

Oil on panel c. 1715-20   45" x 45" (114.3 x 114.3 cms)

Lit: CWAAS Transactions NS Vol. LIII – Calder Abbey by Mary Fair 1953.
         Quarto Magazine, Abbot Hall. Paul Barker. 1986.

Originally the land of Calder Abbey was owned by The Lord of Coupland, Ranulph de Meschines who gave it to the Abbey of Furness under the Order of Savigny. This order merged with the Cistercians in 1147 just over ten years after the monks had begun work on the establishment of Calder Abbey and its grounds.

They were routed by the Scots in 1376 when a second group of monks took charge and tried to persuade Byland Abbey in Yorkshire that Calder was a parent house, but this was refused. It can never have been a very eminent Abbey and when it was suppressed in 1536 it was only valued at £50.9.3¹/₂d. At the Dissolution it was granted to Dr Thomas Leigh by the king, and later it passed to Sir Richard ·Fletcher. It was held by his successors till John Tiffin of Cockermouth bought it in 1724 or 1730. His daughter Sarah married Joseph Senhouse who made considerable alterations to the buildings and surroundings. Much later in the 1880s it passed to the Rymer family who own it to the present time.

There is an engraving by Buck of Calder Abbey 1736 or 1739; the painting was completed some years earlier, possibly about 1730 when John Tiffin bought the property. The latter was probably one of the many local people who commissioned Mathias Read to paint a picture of his estate. Read has chosen the view from the North and includes the original monks entrance or gatehouse. The barns in the foreground have long since gone but the abbey remains much as it appears in the picture painted 260 years ago, except the Western arch which had fallen by the time Buck made the engraving. The present arch is a reconstruction. Mary Fair does not place much reliability on Buck's correctness of detail.[49]

The picture is an example of one of Read's more dramatic paintings. Apart from the fluffy cumulus clouds, edged with light, and being blown in from the west, the ground and wooded hills are painted in dark colours. A further light tonal relief is seen in the translucent paler shades of the tops of the fells behind the Abbey, and on the limestone masonry of the building itself. Its composition is unusual as so often the panels are long and narrow but this picture is exactly square and is devoid of the usual figures in the foreground or elsewhere in the painting. On the top of the hill behind the Abbey is a cluster of buildings no longer there and which appear to be very much out of scale, being too large. The chiaroscuro effect removes this picture from a purely topographical category in a unique way.

Colour plate 6.

VIEW OF LOWTHER.

Lord Cavendish of Furness,
Holker Hall, Cumbria.

Oil on canvas c.1725   35" x 51½" (88.9 x 130.8 cms) B.83/812

This picture was recently described by John Harris as a "sensitive softly-painted landscape with a predominantly green palette. In style it has passages that might have been painted by the Tillemans".[50]

As mentioned in the description of the Lowther painting at Muncaster there are some subtle differences. This version is much more crisply painted than the Muncaster example.

Beyond the sun dappled, undulating foreground is the sweeping vista of fields leading up to Lowther Castle. The fields neatly edged with hedges and dotted with bushes give just enough detail to suggest a well maintained estate and yet denote the rather bleak newly planted environment. A thick band of trees stands on either side of the river, completely separating the foreground from the main part of the picture.

Again it is evident that Read drew inspiration from Jan Wyck in details such as the edging to the clouds with brilliant light. The feeling of recession round the hill to the right is cleverly achieved. Read displays a remarkable evenness of green without its becoming boring. There is a pictorial uniformity in the subtle blue green fields and trees and wide undulating shadows drawn with broad strokes across the canvas. There is nothing timid or fussy in his sweeping lines. The shadow on the hills in the upper left comes down to make a perfect framing of the central theme – the house.

The painting conforms to the strictures of the Netherlandish Bird's Eye school, however it is interesting to notice how he deliberately moved the main features, so as to show the Ullswater mountains. The balance is corrected by featuring the chapel in the foreground. The treatment of the building is reminiscent of Isel seen from the North. With this style he seems to have favoured this proscenium effect.

As late as 1961 this picture was connected with Zuccarelli as so little was known about Mathias Read.[51]

Colour plate 7.

20 Lowther (Muncaster)

VIEW OF LOWTHER.   Mrs P. Gordon-Duff-Pennington,
                                                        Muncaster Castle, Ravenglass.

Oil on Canvas c.1725   32¼" x 47½" (81.9 x 120.5 cms)

Provenance: Brought from Ackworth Park, Yorks.

In 1691 Sir John Lowther reported that "one of the Towers of my house (at Lowther) being ruinous cracked, and the timber rotten" he would have a new one. This was completed well before Celia Fiennes came in 1698 and described it looking "very nobly, with large iron gates into the stable yard, a fine building."

In the month of August 1731, Sir John Clerk who was a Scottish Baronet made an expedition to Cumberland and Westmorland, visiting Lowther to see his son who was at school there.[52] The fact that in his seventy-one pages of manuscript he is eulogistic about much of what he saw at Lowther, does not imply he had no basis for comparison. He was a baronet, who had been born in Scotland, attended Glasgow University, studied law in Leyden and then spent much time on the continent.

He described the seat as he saw it in 1731 with much praise as well as recording that the previous house had been burnt down in 1718, "the beautiful residence of Lord Lonsdale in Westmorland has been entirely destroyed by fire with all its contents".[53]

This impressive view looking directly towards Lowther Castle from a vantage point level with the roof, shows the castle almost in the centre of the canvas set against dark woods, and with the main drive leading up to the entrance gates. Below, to the right is the chapel, over to the right and behind are the hills beyond Ullswater. The Holker picture, is slightly different in that there are three men surveying the vista, instead of two. In the picture, the chapel is shown quite tall, whereas in the Holker picture the chapel has been shown much smaller and hardly rears its head above the band of trees which crosses the foreground. The skies in both paintings are slightly different and in the Muncaster picture an extra white horse is grazing in the far right hand and is rather inclined to draw the eye off the canvas.

Illustrations 20, 21 & 22.

21 Lowther (Muncaster) detail, church

22 Lowther (Muncaster) detail, house

OUSE BRIDGE.   Private Collection.

Oil on panel c.1725   35$^{1/4}$" x 44" (89.5 x 111.7 cms)

Looking over Bassenthwaite Lake, the picture shows its northern end. (Father West was to use this viewpoint as his "second station" on Bassenthwaite some fifty years later.) It gives a panoramic view of the site, with a tree at the right to give a vertical in contrast to the rather flat scene. On the sloping bank in the foreground are two well painted men in tricorne hats sitting on the ground in conversation. One has his left hand raised and his back is curved in a characteristic Read pose. There are many interesting details in the picture such as the old wath at Ouse Bridge, originally known as Ewes Bridge. Mr Wilson remembers in about 1936 the Cumbrian river authority deepened the exit of the lake and during excavations removed the old timbers from the vicinity. These might have been the footing of a bridge. Only a few houses appear in the distance. On the extreme left a boat is tethered and near the long-horned cow a fisherman is pulling in his net. It is painted in cool and muted colours which is in stark contrast to those of his works painted in the evening sun.

The man in the frock coat sitting in the foreground could be Matthew Wane (1643/4–1725). He married his second wife Jane Watson of Cockermouth and a bread cupboard in the Dower House bears the initials M & I W 1692. But as the person seems a fairly young man, the picture probably dates from the first few years of the son Joseph's occupation. This means it could have been painted in about 1725. It may have been ordered to go with the panel paintings in the house to celebrate Joseph's possession of the house. In 1726 Wane carried out renovations and enlargements to the house. The initials of Joseph and his wife Grace, who was a Highmore of Armathwaite Hall, were added over the front door of the Dower House – J. & G. W. A. 1726.

When the family finally parted with the estate in 1831 to Hannah Wane of Armathwaite, a portrait of "Mary's grandfather Matthew Wane" was mentioned – no trace of it has been found but it may well have been by Read.[54]

Although this composition is less satisfactory, it was commissioned to show the view and as such is one of the only known direct landscapes. On the other hand it must be one of the earliest successful landscape paintings by an English hand and is a splendid evocation of the gentle loveliness of Cumbrian countryside.

Colour plate 8.

AN ALLEGORICAL FIGURE ON EITHER   Private Collection.
SIDE OF A ROUND HEADED ARCH.

Oil on panels c.1725   20" x 21" (50.8 x 53.3cm)

In each panel is a seated figure of a woman surrounded with flowers. On the left she is holding a sheaf of wheat and on the right a basket of autumn fruits as if to show a successful conclusion to the farming year. They are decorative scenes of an idyllic nature in imitation of grand wall paintings in large houses. They are much darkened with age, smoke and varnish so that it is hard to make out the colours.

HOUNDS.   Private Collection.

Oil on boards c.1725   5" x 39" (12.7 x 99 cm)

This very narrow picture of hounds is painted on to the panel over a doorway. The hounds are shown simply against rolling hills and clouds and could be otter hounds. Matthew Wane's son Joseph was a keen sportsman and later described as a "gentleman who goes hunting three times a week in that season, if the weather is favourable, and often on foot, he runs stoutly when the dogs are in full cry, though he is 87 years of age; he is one proof of the salutary air, and healthful diet, of this county; and was remarkable for his breed of otter hounds, one of which being sold to Salisbury found its way home again".[55]

This reference to hounds may suggest that those shown in the picture belong to Joseph but appear to be of an earlier date and Matthew probably instigated the pack.

SPRINGTIME FARMING.   Private Collection.

Oil on panel over doorway into the hall and backing the hound panel. c.1725
5" x 39" (12.5 x 99 cms)

This rather simple long narrow arable scene is probably one of the decorative commissions Read carried out.

Four horses and two oxen are drawing a plough guided by a ploughman in white leggings and brown breeches. He wears a cap and it is rare to see a team of different species of animals ploughing in harness together as late as the 18th century. Beside the team another man is dressed in a blue coat and carries a long whip. Behind the plough is a pair of horses harrowing, being led by a farm worker who also appears to have a whip of some description preceeded by a sower 'broadcasting' in the original manner. On the right the scene is being observed by a mounted man who is presumably Joseph Wane. These are perhaps his best studies of cows and horses as they form the principal features of the panel, rather than just being adjuncts.

Illustration 23.

23 Scarness Springtime Farming Mural

CARLISLE FROM STANWIX.   Tullie House Art Gallery, Carlisle.

Oil on panel 1725   35⅛" x 47¾" (89.2 x 121.3 cms)

Provenance: This panel was in the Grapes Inn, Carlisle, and then hung in the Old Town Hall, Carlisle; given to Tullie House 1914. Acc. no. 108 – 1978.157.[56]

The pink sandstone buildings and wall of the town are shown. As was sometimes his custom, Read has not shown the buildings in much detail. Occasionally the grain of the panel shows through the paint which is very thin. The green grass sloping down from the right is probably overcleaned. Faces and figure painting is rather crude. Scotch Gate is shown in the foreground with a sloping bridge. Carrick Fell can be seen behind Carlisle.

The composition of this picture, which suggests it was done after 1720, is most interesting as it foreshadows Richard Wilson's designs of several decades later. The view point has been lowered. The town of Carlisle is a well lit main subject of the work which is "framed" in a typical seventeenth century Roman school manner. On the left are three whimsical freely painted non botanical trees so often seen in Read's paintings. The foreground, which is dark with a road and a few people, runs up a steep shaded escarpment surmounted by the small, gloomy church. A delightful burst of sunlight on the hillside shows the quality of the land, and saves the foreground from dreariness and obscurity. The church and hillock together are nearly two thirds the height of the picture. There is even an expanse of water between the shady foreground and the city; could this be Drught's influence, and if so, how did it reach Whitehaven? It is unusual to see the chatting travellers on the road just about to step out of the corner of the picture – pre-dating Carel Weight!

This elegant composition is so different from his naive early house portraits that it must have been done later in his life. The painter, in apparent isolation, made a long journey and perhaps pointed the way for Dr Syntax.

Colour plate 9.

POOL ON THE RIVER EDEN.   Sir John Lawson, Cumbria.

Oil on canvas c.1725   28³/₄" x 5'2" (73.0 x 157.4 cms)

This wide canvas shows a fisherman, in wig and hat, standing slightly right of centre and fishing in the pool below Corby Castle. This is probably Thomas Howard (1677-1740) who between 1720 and his death spent a third of his income on enriching the environment of the house. His son Philip Howard (1730-1810) was painted by Devis in 1752, and inherited from his father at the early age of ten. The ruins of Wetheral Abbey can be seen on the left. There are two swans in the river and possibly two others alighting on the left. Two figures walk up the opposite bank and three cows are lying near the river. Read's painting shows the caves to the left of the cascade. In front of the caves was a platform and a railing and people could shelter in them and watch the fishing. An elegantly sketched woman leans forward in the shelter and apart from a man in a rowing boat, the picture is rather empty. Indeed the construction of this work is weak and reminiscent of **Ouse Bridge** where the artist has taken the subject matter directly from nature. In this instance Read might have been more successful using one of his more elevated view points so giving the river a sense of continuity.

His early way of handling the trees on the left foreground belies his later management as in **Naworth Castle.** However the great billowing white cumulus clouds against the blue sky gives this painting light, focus, and cohesion. The sky itself is quite different from his usual work and more Roman than Cumbrian and in a way foreshadows those of late Georgian times.

Thomas began laying out the grounds and devising the various additional features in them, such as the cascade, which is clearly shown in the Bucks print of 1739 – **The West View of Wetheral Priory in the County of Cumberland.** The cascade was an ingenious way of collecting up all the water from the adjoining field drains, into a 'head building' and allowing it to flow down the bank, channelled, into a pool below. Whether this structure was as elaborate as indicated by Buck's print is difficult now to verify.

Bolton Art Gallery acquired a lovely drawing (Acc. no: 512) in pen and ink wash, 25.3 x 33.4 cms by Joseph Farrington in 1975. It is called **View of Corby from the Walmon Ware** [Salmon Weir] **lst August 1780.** It shows 3 caves at a lower level and one above. Above the cave is the cascade. Only the 'head' now remains. But there is still a dovecot and other buildings are scattered through the grounds.

Colour plate 10.

24 View of Whitehaven (Tullie House) detail, rustic courtship

25 View of Whitehaven (Tullie House) detail, rustic dancing

VIEW OF WHITEHAVEN.   Tullie House Art Gallery, Carlisle.

Oil on panel Pre 1710   34³/₄" x 47⁵/₈" (88.3 x 121.9 cm)

Provenance: The Grapes Inn was built as a private house, possibly for the Carlisle Spedding family. This, one of three known panels, was probably commissioned by Spedding. Acc.no. 108-1978. 177.

Undulating hills, under a pinkish sky with white cumulus clouds set off Whitehaven lying snugly in the valley. The hills are very green with strong dark shadows, contrasting with the very pale blue water of the bay, where the ships are sketchily drawn in the distance. An extraordinary small red and yellow band in the left foreground defies interpretation.

In the foreground a party of four pairs of bucolic people are carousing under two trees. They, with rather mask-like faces, sit huddled together, a spilt pitcher at their feet. In an adjoining group two people are dancing and three others stand watching a fiddler playing. Three cows also join in, one licking up the spilt milk. Two further cows, a little way off, are used rather clumsily, to create an illusion of depth between the edge of the foreground hill and the middle distance where again a group of people and cows are shown, but this time extremely small. The details of costume are good. All this rural jollity enlivens an otherwise rather plain picture. It differs enormously from the four other portraits of Whitehaven in its construction as a general picture, with the eye drawn to the town of Whitehaven.

The style of painting is broad, with refreshing patches of light and shade – which are very well handled. It is difficult to believe that Read was not influenced by pictures of Lakes Albano, and Nemi. A grey spire not previously recorded, appears on the church in the centre, but recently documentary evidence for it has come to light.

The dating of this picture is particularly important as it would appear to be one of the earliest he painted in Whitehaven. There is only one pier in the harbour which would suggest 1690-1706. There are only six to ten ships in all in the harbour and later in the century we hear of the great numbers of ships which used to be seen. There is no cutting for the mine track railway. The town is still relatively small and the painting of people and animals suggest an early date.

Colour plate 11. Illustrations 24 & 25.

A PROSPECT OF WHITEHAVEN
FROM BRACKENTHWAITE.

Yale Center for British Art,
Newhaven, Conn.

Oil on canvas c.1730   40" x 72" (101.6 x 182.8 cms)

Provenance: Formerly the property of the Rt. Hon. the Earl of Lonsdale by family descent. Entered in a Sotheby's Sale 27 Nov. 1974, Lot 49. It was bought by Christopher Gibbs, New Bond Street, and sold to Paul Mellon, in 1976.

This picture is recorded in the will of Sir William Lowther, who died in 1756 and was amongst the 144 works listed by Hinde and removed from Flatt Hall to Holker Hall. Hinde suggests the date 1730.

This extensive view of Whitehaven shows Flatt Hall and its walled park to the left, in the distant centre is St Nicholas Church. Mr Hay thought the picture was painted between 1730 when the lighthouse on the Old Quay was moved, and 1735 when the Merchant's Tongue quay, not shown in this view, was completed. This view was to be painted at least four more times before it was engraved by R. Parr in 1739 from one version.

Here also the wonderfully planned grid system, carried out from the 1680s by the Lowther family is recorded. Built to cope with the fast expanding coal industry and to house the ever increasing numbers of workers, the town reached its zenith in the mid eighteenth Century.

Here can be seen the blast furnace in the hills, the track in the foreground for the use of rope walkers. There are ships loading coal in the harbour. In the distance there is a clear view of the Isle of Man. Perhaps as in no other contemporary picture it illustrates how the Industrial Revolution was going to change the face of the English countryside by the introduction of its straight hard lines and its regimental planning.

John Harris describes it as "without peer among oil-painted views of English towns. Its date brings it right into the cartographic tradition and in this alone Read finds a small place among Rigaud or Rocque, or even, considering his view was engraved and therefore available for general consumption in London, as a painter anticipating the urban topography of the age of Scott".[57]

Colour plate 12.

A PROSPECT OF WHITEHAVEN. Lord Cavendish of Furness,
Holker Hall, Cumbria.

Oil on canvas c.1730-3   42½" x 72½" (105.4 x 184.1 cms)
(Photograph by courtesy of Courtauld Institute)

Provenance: This painting was originally at Whitehaven but among those sent to
Holker Hall in September 1757 by the Will of Sir William Lowther.

Research done by the late Daniel Hay suggests the date of 1733. Although it bears
a label with a date which appears to be 1738, subject matter suggested it was
earlier. It shows the cutting for the waggon way built between 1733 -34. But it does
not show Merchant's Quay which was built in 1732 so it is thought to be the even
earlier date of 1730. (Merchant's Quay was later known as Old Tongue, then
Sugar Tongue and now Fish Quay.)

Again it shows the grid-iron system of the town-planning scheme with open
spaces rapidly becoming gardens for the mansions set in their midst, built for the
well-to-do who were developing the town. But there are differences. An interesting
excerpt from a letter from the late Richard Cavendish to Daniel Hay summarizes
these, between his painting and the Whitehaven Museum version[58]:-

"In our picture the harbour is a very different shape and there are no large
ships at all. There are a series of small boats going off into the horizon as I have
illustrated and you will notice that the windmill has shifted position considerably.
In the background the shape of the fields differ widely and in the middle
foreground there is a large grey horse and to its left is a stone dated 1738."

This differs from the Yale picture in the foreground, the cattle and men have
been re-arranged as they gaze at the town. In the middle distance Read's usual
array of tiny animals and figures give the sense of scale and recession. It has been
described as a 'slighter version' but apart from the greater abundance of life in the
Mellon picture all these versions sustain a great quality. It is painted in subdued
pale bluey-green. The houses are hard edged with tiny wedge shaped shadows of
the chimneys on the roofs. It has several of his long flowing worm-like broad brush
strokes as in the field in front of the windmill. The horizontal bands of clouds in
Read's strong sky emphasise the structure of the spreading town. The red stone
walls round the Hall gardens are conspicuous in this version. The whole picture
has a clinical effect with its hard lines and sparsely populated streets, although a
few tiny figures may be espied in the streets near the Flatts. Behind the Flatts the
row of houses which appears in the Askham version is not shown in this one.

John Harris thinks that passages almost resemble Tillemans and speculates
upon a possible link between Read and Tillemans, for as he points out there were
two Tillemans in the Sir John Lowther Collection – **A View of Furness Abbey** in
water colours and **A Horse and a Groom**.[59]

Colour plate 13.

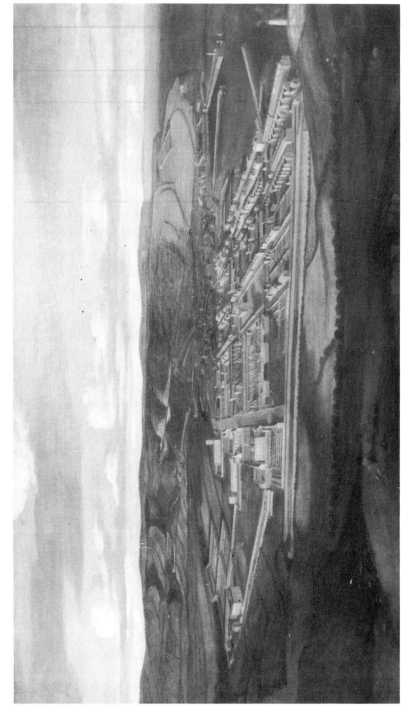

26 A Prospect of Whitehaven (Askham Hall)

A PROSPECT OF WHITEHAVEN.
The Earl of Lonsdale,
Askham Hall, Cumbria.

Oil on canvas c.1734-5   41" x 71" (104.1 x 180.3 cms)

Provenance: This picture descended with **A Prospect of Whitehaven from Brackenthwaite,** now in the Mellon Collection by family descent to the present owner and originally came from Flatt Hall in Whitehaven.

A strong clue to its dating is the appearance of Merchant's Quay suggesting a date after the previous two pictures.

The windmill is shown and the waggon way is there.

In tones of colour it is more akin to the Holker and Mellon versions than to that at Whitehaven Museum. Of all the versions this is more of a picture and less of a plan than the others. The sky though beautiful is more serene and he has managed to achieve a more rounded composition in spite of the man made structures with which he is confronted.

Illustration 26.

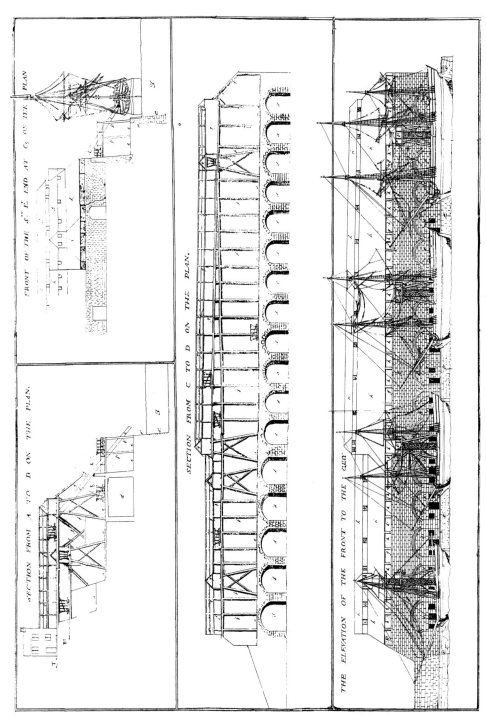

FRONT OF THE S.E. END AT C ON THE PLAN

SECTION FROM A TO B ON THE PLAN.

SECTION FROM C TO D ON THE PLAN.

THE ELEVATION OF THE FRONT TO THE QUAY

27 Plans of "The Hurries"

66

A BIRD'S EYE VIEW OF WHITEHAVEN.   Whitehaven Museum, Cumbria.

Oil on canvas c. 1735   40" x 70" (101.6 x 177.8 cms)

Whitehaven Museum acquired this splendid version of the view of Whitehaven in 1981 with grants from the Victoria & Albert Museum and National Art Collections Fund. The Museum has collected artefacts from the coal industry, and tobacco, spirits and sugar trades from the New World. It also has a fine collection of portraits of the original creators of the town, the Lowther family and other dignitaries.

As with the other pictures of Whitehaven, the foreground is dominated by the long line of the rope-walk where the hemp ropes for shipping and mine haulage were manufactured. There are fewer figures but the windmill is shown, and painted a dark colour as opposed to the white of the Askham version. Merchant's Quay had been built. But the town still has the freshness of its early formative years; the gardens have not yet been filled with additional houses; and there is still the idealism of the dream town so it is possible that this painting was no later than 1735. In the park of Flatt Hall were gardens emulating Versailles with springs and fountains. The "Flatts Walks" is a modern reminder; one of the original sources of water to provide a drinking tap is still there today.

On the far right, the old town is painted in dull colours in order to show off the new. Flatt Hall is on the extreme left. Somerset House is still there with its turret and the prominent rope walk in front of it. The two Churches, Holy Trinity and St Nicholas, are there. (Later St James was to be built near the position of the artist when he painted the view.) Behind the harbour is the "Hurries" whence the coal was loaded to the ships below on a system of gravity loading, the coal coming down constantly through open shoots leading straight to the waiting vessels. The "Hurries" was 115 yards by 19 yards and described as consisting of "17,480 cubic yards and at $3^3/_8$ cubic yards to the waggon will contain 5244 waggons of coals".[60]

In this painting Read shows great confidence in his use of colour, in the composition and in his handling of the figures, his ease and competence is shown both in the large foreground people and the very small distant men in the town streets. It differs from the others in the great attention to detail of the individual houses and gardens, even down to newly planted bushes and trees.

The problem of uniting the angular town with the freely painted undulating countryside has been masterfully overcome. This has partially been achieved by the peripheral use of darker colour, as in the deep shadow of foreground and left side, dark patches of the sea and the sombre grey clouds in both top corners. The composition is fulfilled by his skilful use of light in illuminating the buildings and making the focal point of the design. Despite the profusion of detail this does not detract from its being one of his most successful works.

Colour plate 14.   67

VIEW OF WHITEHAVEN PORT.   Whitehaven Museum, Cumbria.

Oil on canvas c.1715   25¹/₂" x 48¹/₄" (64.7 x 122.2 cms)

This picture was painted before the Old Tongue and New Tongue Quays were built, so probably can be dated to about 1715 when the ships were becoming more numerous. Its long narrow format gives a view of Whitehaven painted from the south shore of the basin. The panorama shows the harbour, shipping and the town both old and new. Behind are the hills with fields and farms.

In the foreground the ships and rigging are accurately portrayed; indeed on one beached ship the seamen are removing the sails from the yards. The bollards, which can still be seen on the quay, were in full use. Also on the quayside there are well painted stevedors amongst the unshipped cannons. Contrasting with the predominant yellowish-brown of the foreground, the cream and pink houses of the town are brightly lit and have local blue-grey slate roofs. His handling of the light on the Old Town houses is masterful, with lovely modulations of light. All the main buildings are clearly identifiable but this picture differs from all the others of Whitehaven in that it is made from a low viewpoint. In the centre is a small area where coal has been piled.

Read clearly depicts the well hedged narrow fields which seem to have been pasture. The rolling hills surround scattered farmsteads and a quarry. All this is surmounted by one of the artist's earlier attempts to portray cumulus clouds against a hazy blue sky.

Colour plate 15. Illustration 28.

28 View of Whitehaven Port

VIEW OF PARTON.   Michael and Sylvia Moon,
                                                                       Whitehaven.

Oil on boards 1700-1708   22$^{1/2}$" x 42$^{1/4}$" (57.1 x 106.9 cms)

This **View of Parton** is painted from the North. It shows the breakwater and a few large houses, with the eroding cliffs going towards Whitehaven. It is an early painting. A ship is sailing out from Whitehaven, which is hidden behind the first headland. It is painted in the clear light of evening which he so often used. The house on the top of the hill, overlooking Parton, is Briscoe Bank once the Black Cock – an inn with a cockpit.[61]

The strong satisfying composition is bold and simple, animated by the usual scattering of figures and cattle in the foreground. There are also people and horses on the pier who are painted very small so as to give an apparent distance. There used "to be a wooden pier at Parton, restored as early as 1695 by the Lamplugh family".[62] The painting seems to show the breakwater as being rebuilt of stone which may date from this restoration. Two red roof-tops relieve the restrained colours of the dark green cliff tops, and convincing purple swirling beach; this purple colouring is the result of the underlying coal and is the same today. The angular houses and bluffs are shown in strong light and shade whilst the light scudding clouds are almost luminous. Although very freely painted Read shows deft handling of his foreground figures and the ships lying beside the wharf. This ability is also used to show fine lines of light edging the stone work.

The house on the extreme left and the sailing ship, the remains of which are just visible on the extreme right, seem to have been added as an attempt to strengthen the composition. As the house differs in colour and perspective from the rest of the picture it may even have been added by a different hand. Parton has an interesting history. Its harbour was important, but its wooden pier collapsed in the 1630s and owing to rivalry between William Fletcher and Sir John Lowther over the pits and ports used by each, it was not restored for some time. In 1695 Sir John Lowther allowed Thomas Lamplugh to build on the old foundations and to construct a pier to allow up to ten vessels. Further work was carried out on it by Sir James, who succeeded Sir John in 1706. In the gale of November 1718 Parton pier was destroyed again and there followed six years of legal battle over its construction.[63]

There was a glasshouse (glass factory) at Parton founded in 1719 but it only lasted until 1721.[64] The Whitehaven glasshouse was built by the Lowthers and lasted from 1735-42 and supplied Belfast, Dublin, Norway, and many towns on the south coast of Scotland as well as neighbouring Lancaster, with bottles.

Colour plate 16.

29 Ship on a rough sea

30 Man on a white horse

SHIP ON A ROUGH SEA.
Richard Walker, Esq.,
The Lowther Arms, Parton.

Oil on panel c.1700   13⅝" x 28½" (34.6 x 72.3 cms)

The Inn used to belong to the Lowthers and there is little doubt that upper rooms were once used by visitors to the town when it was at its prime. In this upper room are three paintings above an old fireplace. These pictures have been in the smokey room for nearly three hundred years and are remarkably well preserved in the circumstances. The three vertical marks on the surface of **Abraham and Isaac** are the singe marks of candle flames, used for two hundred years as the light source. Both the left and right hand panels have traces of once being used as cupboard doors. This one has a key hole and handle and the panel on the right still retains its early hinges.

On the left is a brig, in imminent danger aback and under shortened sail in a rough sea against dark clouds flushed with pink light. The Lowther Arms played its part in smuggling, and apparently there used to be a signal to ships from the hill behind. This ship may bear some reference to those activities. But it appears to be a collier brig and therefore could have been carrying coal. Brigs were also responsible for bringing in most of the tobacco imports. To the right there seems to be a smaller ship wrecked on the rocks.

Illustration 29.

MAN ON A WHITE HORSE.
Richard Walker, Esq.,
The Lowther Arms, Parton.

Oil on board c.1700   14" x 25¼" (35.5 x 64.1 cms)

The second picture, on the right, shows a man in a red coat and on a white horse which is rearing. A second rider comes up from the left, on a chestnut mount. They appear to be gesticulating towards the river where two men are also staring in front of them and pointing. The background seems more like a theatrical set, and up on a jagged mountain ledge is what looks like a castle with a Pele Tower. A bright yellow sky adds a sense of expectation to the scene.

In the lower left of the painting is the device Read often used, two trees which intercross.

Illustration 30.

71

31 William Gibson

32 Abraham and Isaac

WILLIAM GIBSON. (1699-1745)   Private Collection.

Oil on canvas c.1730   29" x 24" (73.6 x 60.9 cms)

William Gibson was the father of Mary Gibson. "His brother was the Rev. Thomas Gibson, (1695-1745) Prebendary of Peterborough. His Aunt Elizabeth married Mathias Read. William Gibson married Margaret Hind and had a son William born 1733 and Mary born 1734 and who afterwards married James Hale. They had one son William who settled in Virginia and a daughter Elizabeth born 1778, who married first Captain Braithwaite and then my great great grandfather John Piele".[65] This quotation comes from the diary of a Miss Peile one of the owner's forbears, and is quoted in full because of the connection through marriage with Read.

William sits impassively staring slightly to his right. His left hand is tucked into his waistcoat and he wears a trim wig. He is painted in a cartouche. The technique shows competent handling of the paint. His features are well managed certainly more convincingly than the treatment of the folds in the textiles.

Illustration 31.

ABRAHAM and ISAAC.   Richard Walker, Esq.,
                                                  The Lowther Arms, Parton.

Oil on boards c.1700 $27^{1}/_{2}$" x $40^{1}/_{8}$" (69.8 x 101.7 cms)

This is the central panel over the fireplace. It is an ambitious rendering of the biblical story of Abraham in the act of sacrificing his son Isaac to God, when suddenly an Angel stays his hand and stops him. Abraham is shown pressing his son's head down with his left hand. Isaac lies awkwardly, his hands tied behind his back. The Angel appears like a swift arrow out of grey turbulent cloud and seizes Abraham's right arm. A strange dog-like ram is hovering on the right in front of a caldron containing a flaming fire, ready for the sacrifice. The red stain on the ground probably denotes a place of sacrifice. Away below is a distant landscape, not unlike that from Mount Hermon today. The human group may appear to be painted inside the mouth of a cave, but it may be just rock and tree behind them. The portrayal of Abraham is well rendered with a strong patriarchal face and sound anatomical construction. The angel has quite a good face but the way Isaac is treated is less convincing. It would be very interesting to see this picture after restoration.

Illustration 32.

34 Joe Hinde

33 Mary Gibson

MARY GIBSON. (aged three).   Private Collection.

Oil on canvas. 1737   29" x 24$^{1}/_{2}$" (73.6 x 62.2 cms)

Mary was the daughter of William Gibson.

This and the portrait of her father descended through the Peile family to their present owner. It is described, by the nineteenth Century diarist Miss Peile as "our great, great grandmother".[65]

She is sitting rather stiffly against a rural background, and draped in a flowing robe, both this and her expression make her look older. Again the face is well painted. One of Read's characteristics in his portraits is the way his sitters stare with rather dark untwinkling eyes and pursed lips. Her bodice is caught with a central brooch and she could be taken for a young teenager.

Illustration 33.

JOE HINDE.   Private Collection.

Oil on canvas c.1740   35$^{1}/_{2}$" x 27" (90 x 68.6 cms)

Ex.1982   "Four Hundred Years of Cumbrian Painting" Abbot Hall Art Gallery, Cat. No. 11

The portrait is of a young boy and has come down through Read's descendants, as did those of Mary and William Gibson. On the reverse of the canvas is a label "said to have been a gambler".

This picture was exhibited in the "Four Hundred Years of Cumbrian Painting" exhibition organised at Abbot Hall in 1982.[66]

The style of Read's treatment of textile can be seen clearly in this picture. The folds are shown with no particular skill in the subtleties of tone, or fine gradations of shadow. The touches of light on the cuffs of his shirt are more successful. He has a calculating look in his eye.

The picture was so dark in the time of the diarist that it was thought by the family that the boy was holding a bright Victorian penny, which he'd had as a tip – in fact it was the dog's eye.[67]

Illustration 34.

36 Mary Littledale

35 Joseph Littledale

76

JOSEPH LITTLEDALE. 1714-1744   Private Collection.

Oil on canvas. c.1738-40   28¹/₄" x 23¹/₄" (72.3 x 59.6 cms)

Joseph Littledale and his wife Mary were residents of West Cumbria. The portraits have descended through the family to their present owner and are well painted, giving an air of individuality about the sitters.

He wears a golden brown jacket with gold buttons, and a wig and is holding a book in his right hand. The colouring is warm and rich which brings out the sitter's character.

Illustration 35.

MARY LITTLEDALE. (n Langton) 1714/1754   Private Collection.

Oil on canvas. c.1738-40   28³/₈" x 23¹/₂" (71.8 x 57.6 cms)

Mary is wearing a pale cream silk dress with pink ribbons in her bodice and has a bright pink shawl to match, over her left arm. This, and the portrait of her husband is painted on a dark ground. It is a sensitive portrait and well above the standard of most provincial limners. Again there is in Read's painting of the eyes a certain recognisable characteristic.

The late Daniel Hay attributed these to Mathias Read.

Illustration 36.

37 Last Supper (Crosscanonby)

THE LAST SUPPER.   Crosscanonby Church.

Oil on board c.1717   42" x 56½" (107 x 143.5 cms)

In the Church of Crosscanonby hangs a painting, of the Last Supper, hitherto by an unknown artist. It is in all probability by Mathias Read.

Unfortunately a known Last Supper by Read was destroyed by the fire of 1971 at St Nicholas Church, Whitehaven. There is little resemblance between the two, as far as one can see from the very poor photograph which exists of the St Nicholas version.

Although there is no halo shown round the head of Christ, as in the Whitehaven painting, his head is shown against an alcove to give the same effect. The young man coming in on the right of the picture is probably John Mark. He is bearing a pitcher and his head is averted.

There are similarities between the faces of the apostles and Read's known works at Kirkby Ireleth Church. Crosscanonby was the family church of the Senhouse family and Humphrey Senhouse was for some time a patron.

It was cleaned two years ago, revealing brilliant colour. Jesus is wearing a red cloak over a white undergarment. The disciple with his back turned to us has a bright orange undergarment and red cloak. John Mark is in brown and the man with his elbow on the table is in yellow and blue. There is a pink sky outside and a single silver cup stands on a greyish cloth.

Illustration 37.

Details of two church paintings, of which no pictorial record exists, follow for comparison:

THE ASCENSION. Formerly at Holy Trinity Church, Whitehaven.

c. 1713-15

An altar piece was painted by Read for this Church, and we do not know whether this was a commission or a donation by the artist as he donated £10 towards the building fund in 1713. No drawing or record of this painting remains.

THE LAST SUPPER. Formerly at St Nicholas Church, Whitehaven.

Oil on boards. c.1713

This painting, an altar piece, was commissioned by Elisha Gale in 1708 and carried out in the next few years, the exact date is not known. It was a tremendous success and encouraged many more commissions not least the pictures of Moses and Aaron referred to elsewhere. But even the poor photograph which is all that remains of the altar piece, shows more vitality in the painting than is evident by the heavily 'touched up' pictures of Moses and Aaron. A contemporary describes it, however, as "lacking conviction in the figure of Christ which is the worst feature of the painting". It is framed in an ornate manner flanked by urns and within the curving broken pediment is the dove symbolic of the holy spirit. Two roses are on either side. The words 'This do in remembrance of me' follow the curve of the top of the frame, described in Caine's **Churches of Whitehaven Rural Deanery 1916**, as semicircular.

At all events it has gone. From the photograph it appears to have been a fairly vigorous picture containing Christ in conversation with his disciples closely seated round a table. An open book and two candlesticks stand on a shelf to the right and provide the only light sources. Most of the disciples are watching Christ intently. There is a strong similarity between these figures and those on the Parton panel paintings.

The last reference to it was in 1916 when it had been taken down from the apse in the clergy vestry where it was described as being in danger. Finally it was destroyed in the fire of St Nicholas Church in 1971.

MOSES AND AARON.   St James Church,
                                                                    Whitehaven.

These two large paintings by Read were commissioned to enhance his successful Last Supper at St Nicholas Church. They survived the fire and in the last few years were put into the newly arranged gallery of St James Church where they stand now in the S.E. corner of the right hand gallery. Both have suffered much by retouching by 'house painters' over the years but retain a few of the characteristics of Read. Large and striking from a distance they still show those features for which they were designed – to be imposing from afar.

These figures were a common sight in Churches in the eighteenth century as Hilda Gamlin indicated, about a picture project in St Paul's Cathedral, Covent Garden, in 1773, "Moses and Aaron upon a church wall holding up the commandments for fear they should fall".[68]

38 Moses. St James, Whitehaven   39 Aaron. St James, Whitehaven

MOSES.

St James Church,
Whitehaven.

Oil on boards c.1720   92" x 39¹/₂" (203 x 103 cms)

Moses stands on the left and holds the tablets, depicted as long and rounded at the top, in his left hand. On one can be read Exodus, and on the other is an attempt to show the title in Greek or Aramaic. The text is simulated writing and not decipherable. In his right hand he holds a twig or rod with buds. He is shown with flowing grey hair and beard, standing on a pedestal against a dark brown background. Over his yellow undergarment there is a sandy brown cloak with a red scarf.[69]

Illustration 38.

AARON.

St James Church,
Whitehaven.

Oil on board c.1720   92" x 39¹/₂" (203 x 103 cms)

Against a dark brown background, Aaron stands out in equally vibrant colours. He has a reddish brown beard and wears a gold brown mitre. Correctly speaking he should be wearing a dome shaped hat. He has an ornate red chasuble and a red kinquare over a white cassock. The lower edge of his upper garment has golden tassels suspended from it. He also stands on a pedestal. A great breastplate in a gold frame the Urim and Thummin hangs from a chain round his neck. The brightly painted 'jerkin' over his 'surplice' is in red, gold and blue and is probably intended to show embroidery but it is hard to decide what materials are depicted because of constant retouching over the last 260 years.

Illustration 39.

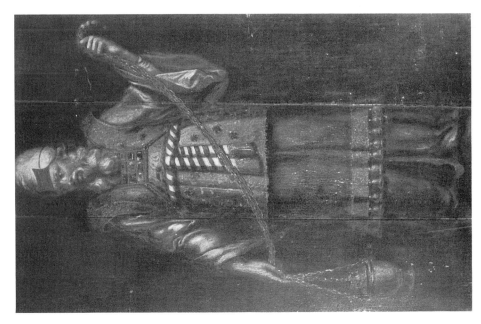

41 Aaron St Cuthbert's, Kirby Ireleth

40 Moses. St Cuthbert's, Kirby Ireleth

84

MOSES. St Cuthbert's Church,
Kirkby Ireleth.

Oil on board c.1720   49" x 31" (124.5 x 78.7 cms)

He is wearing an enveloping garment. The book of the law stands behind him, and on his feet are leather sandals. He is carrying his rod and he points his right finger upwards as if perhaps to say that there is only one God.

Illustration 40.

AARON. St Cuthbert's Church,
Kirkby Ireleth.

Oil on boards c.1720   49" x 31" (124.5 x 78.7 cms)

Aaron is wearing the high priest's dress and breastplate. This plate was divided into 12 squares, each representing one of the tribes of Israel. To it was attached the Urim and Thummin, oracles consulted before battle when the King would ask God through the High Priest whether Israel would be victorious. They were not used after the destruction of the first Temple. He holds a censer.

This pair has suffered less from the hands of retouchers. The treatment of textiles and voluminous garments is typically Readian. The successful compositions and the convincing stance of the two figures show some improvement on the Whitehaven pair.

These two panels at Kirkby Ireleth can certainly be attributed to Mathias Read.

Illustration 41.

ROYAL ARMS IN CHURCHES OF WEST CUMBRIA.

As mentioned in the text Mathias Read painted the Royal Arms for Whitehaven and Penrith. It seemed possible he might have been responsible for others in the area. Of those listed in an article by the late Bruce Thompson[70] only those between 1693 and 1747, when Read died, had to be inspected. They were:-

Aspatria	A R 1711
Bromfield	G R I
Crosscanonby	G II R 1733
Isel	G R I 1714
Millom	G R I 1714
Morland	G R I 1714
Penrith (St Andrews)	G R 1723
Threlkeld	G R I 1714
Troutbeck	G R II 1737
Whitbeck	A R 1707-1714
Whitehaven (St Nicholas)	W III R 1693
Whitehaven (Holy Trinity)	G R I 1715
Witherslack	A R 1710

A further list of those in existence in 1967 but not hung, was recorded, e.g. Torpenhow whose arms have now alas disappeared.

From a careful photographic survey of the above thirteen it is possible, with confidence, to attribute some to Mathias Read on stylistic grounds. The one at Whitehaven known to be by Read is in good condition and has not been badly touched up or repainted. It gives therefore accurate and clear information.

The **Arms at Whitehaven** (now in St Nicholas Church), 65½" x 75½" (166.3 x 191.7 cms), is on boards running vertically. The colour is fresh and there are good gradations of light and shade giving a strong three dimensional appearance. Lettering is finely executed and the initials W R and M R denoting the reign of William and Mary appear on the upper left and right. It was painted in 1693.

At **St Andrews Church, Penrith**, 61" x 86" (154.9 x 218.4 cms), Mathias Read painted and dated the Arms in 1723 in the reign of George I. If this was not a known fact it would have been difficult to attribute it to Read. All surfaces have been painted over with flat, dull and opaque colours and none of Read's original liveliness remains. The light in the animals' eyes has disappeared as have the highlights on the lion's claws. The shackling and mane of the unicorn have become incorporated into a metal headpiece joining the collar.

St Michael & All Angels Church, Isel, 27¼" x 34¼" (69 x 90 cms) This is a much smaller arms painted on boards running horizontally, but it has all the freshness, colour and vitality of Read's hand as seen at Whitehaven in the arms now in St Nicholas Church. It is not overpainted and the lettering is Read's, It is dated 1714, in the reign of George I.
Illustration 42.

St Kentigern's Church, Aspatria, retains the Arms of Anne, dated 1711 47¼" x 47¼" (120 x 120 cms), there is enough stylistic similarity to attribute it to Read. It is painted on horizontal boards, and bears the initials A R.

St Mungo's Church, Bromfield, has the arms to George I , 43¼" x 43¼" (109.9 x 109.9 cms), and is painted on six panels joined horizontally. It very much resembles the other arms painted by Read.

At **St John's Church, Crosscanonby,** 34¼" x 37" (86.8 x 92.8 cms) the arms are to George II. They are very hard to see and are painted on boards laid vertically. The panel has a rounded central top. The Church was that of the Senhouse family. After photographing it in a good light it is attributed with confidence to Read.

42 Royal Arms, Isel Church

THE LAST BOAR, or THE BOAR HUNT.   M. Falcon, Esq.,
                                                Kirkland House, Loweswater.

Oil paint on panel c.1710   1'8½" x 2'7½" (52.00 x 80 cms)

This is a curious painting with very interesting connotations. First of all it represents a man and hounds attacking a boar. The last boar in the wild had become extinct in 1683. Others were kept in captivity for some time after that. Secondly the hounds shown are not suitable for hunting boar, where proper boarhounds, heavy mastiffs, were used. The hounds shown here appear to be 'valuable' dogs and perhaps they are being shown as 'superdogs'. Apart from this the spear should have a narrower blade and cross-piece set further back from the point.[71] All in all these details lead one to believe it is probably painted from imagination or based on an earlier picture, possibly after Snyder. Such was the romance of the subject that Read could have painted it from stories of the last Boar Hunts. Added to this the studied expression of the hunter makes it look like a retrospective picture. Dogs do not normally line up, but spread out to keep the boar's attention while one of them runs in to grab it by the flank. The dogs are well done. Read had often painted dogs and hounds, but the boar and young look stiff and wooden.

Illustration 43.

43 Boar Hunt

REYNARD TRIUMPHANT. (Fox & Wild Cats)   Tullie House Art Gallery,
after Frans Snyder   Carlisle.

Oil on panel c.1730   25" x 42½" (63.5 x 107.9 cm)

Acc. no: 6 – 1914.7

Label: Reynard 'Triumphant' School of Frans Snyders June 1898

Provenance: This is the third panel from the Grapes Inn; hung in Old Town Hall until transferred to Tullie House in 1914.

The fox is in the act of killing a hen and there are three cats snarling at the fox. There is a ruined castle in the background and water in the distance. It is all painted in browns, golds and dun colours, bar the brilliant red of the cat's eyes, the blood red on the hen's head and chest and the gold eyes of the cat on the right.

In the lower left are three large leaves commonly used in pictures as a device to frame the scene. Behind the little group a rather strange tree root system and trunks rear up as a background but the paint is thin after drastic cleaning. However the quality of the painting of the fox in particular is very competent.

References to this and **Carlisle from Stanwix** and **View of Whitehaven**; are found in Carlisle Journals and their subsequent fate can be followed.[72]

Illustration 44.

44 Reynard Triumphant

"*The Indenture made the Thirty first day of October in the thirteenth year of the reign of our souveraign Lord William the Third by the grace of God of England and Scotland France Ireland King defender of the Faith Anno domini 1701—— Between the Honorable Sir John Lowther of Whitehaven in the County of Cumberland Barronett of the one part and Mathias Reed of Whitehaven aforesaid Painter of the other part Witneffeth the said Sir John Lowther for in consideration of the sum of five shillings of lawfull money of England to him in hand paid by the said Mathias Reed off and before the delivery of these —— the receipt whereof he doth hereby acknowledge and thereof and of every part thereof doth acquit and discharge the said Mathias Reed his —— and —— of thence for ever by these present hath bargained sold —— and confirmed and by those present for him and his kind doth bargain sell —— and confirm unto the said Matthias Reed his kind and —— All that parts of ground lying and being in Whitehaven aforesaid on the North side of a street there called Irish Street and containing in FFront towards the —— lately erected by the said Sir John Lowther (the said ffront —— in a lyne with the —— and —— buildings of the south part of James Tyson's house in James Street in the said town of Whitehaven)*"

		£	s	d
"A Cummulation of the Painting work to be don in ye Parish Church of Penrith as follows				
The Cornnifh Round the top 12 yards at two shilling a yard don with foliage in the frize and bulks between the Medillions and gilding the Rings in the Caps of the Pillars		12	0	0
The Body's of the Pillars don Stone Couler at three shillings per pillar		03	0	0
The Altar piece painted with any Story Shall be thought fitt not exceeding twenty figures		20	0	0
The wood Arch Painted stone Couler the spandrills and pannills filld with such figures as shall be thought fitt don in Stone Coulers		06	0	0
	totall	41	0	0

All Conveniances and Assistence for scafolding to be found at the expence of the Parish

		£	s	d
The numbering the seats with gold ground and a hansom compartment about them at 6d pr seat 200 seats		5	0	0
the stones don oaken Coulers and Graine		1	0	0
The Gold to be found by the Painter for the Caps of the Pillars		4	10	0
the Rails above the Altar		0	10	0

June 30th 1722

I doe agree to execute the above painting for forty six pounds be witness my hand

MATH READ"

45 Dr Brownrigg by Edward Alcock

Portrait of Dr Brownrigg. *(1711-1800)*

Edward Alcock. Oil on Canvas 28¹/₂" x 23¹/₂" (72.5 x 59.6 cms)

Dr Brownrigg was born in 1711 at High Close Hall, Bassenthwaite. After being trained as an Apothecary in Carlisle in 1730, he went to Leyden for a course in medicine along with many leading medical figures of the day. He graduated in 1737 and returned immediately to practise medicine in Whitehaven. He visited patients from Carlisle to Cockermouth and to Millom in the south of the county. He was a Physician as opposed to a Surgeon.

When he treated Read in 1747 he had been practising for ten years but it is not likely that the portrait was painted at the beginning of his career. The style of the furniture suggests a somewhat later date. He turned away from medicine and worked more and more in the field of scientific research, looking at the subject of fire damp in the mines among other problems.[73]

Brownrigg was an important member of an intellectual coterie which included John Dalton of Dean, poet and divine, John Brown D.D. theologian author and artist from Wigton and the Gilpin family. He was tutor to William in the 1770s.

He appears to have been about 49 in the painting. It must have been painted between 1757-60 and is in all probability the work of Edward Alcock of Birmingham and Bristol. The latter was a peripatetic artist and miniaturist. His small formal portraits were in the manner of Devis and he is known to have flourished from 1757-1778. From 1763-1774 his work was normally signed and dated.[74]

Illustration. 45.

Mathias Read's Will

"In the Name of God, Amen, I Mathias Read of Whitehaven in the County of Cumberland Painter being at present indisposed but of sound & perfect Mind Memory and Understanding Do make Publish and Declare this my last Will and Testament in manner & form following, First I give Devise & Bequeath unto my Dearly beloved Wife Elizabeth Read, All my Messuages Lands Tenements and Hereditaments whatsoever in Whitehaven aforesaid within the Parish of Saint Bees in the said County of Cumberland And all my Estate Right Tithes and

Inter–law or in Equity Reversion & Reversions Remainder and Remainders whatsoever of in into or out of all or any Messuages Lands Tenements or Hereditaments within the sd Parish of Saint Bees to hold to for the said Elizabeth for & during the term of her Natural life and from and after her demise I give & Deliver the same unto my Worthy Friends William Gale & Peter Gale both of Whitehaven aforsd Merchants their Heirs & assigners for ever to sell Dispose thereof as they shall think fit for the best advantage for the Uses hereafter mentioned, Also I give and bequeath to the said William Gale & Peter Gale Each the sum of Ten Pounds to be raised & deducted out of the Messuages arising by the sale of my said Real Estate after my said Wifes Demise Also all the said residue & remainder of All said Messuages shall be raised by sale & my said Real Estate as aforesaid I give & bequeath unto my loving sister Mary Dennis of her two daughters my Nephew William Wood to be Equally Divided amongst them Also I give & bequeath to my nephew Ambrose Wood the sum of two shillings & sixpense Also I give bequeath to my said Wife Elizabeth the sum of Fifty pounds Also I give Devise and bequeath to my said wife Elizabeth all those my seats or pews in the New Church in Whitehaven aforesaid to hold the same to her or Heirs Exuctors administrators & assigned according to the Terms in the original Instrument of Subscription for–ing the said Church Also I give and bequeath to my sister Mary Dennis the sum of Tenpounds to be raised & paid by my Executors hereafter named out of my personall Estate in case my sd sister Mary survives me but in case she shall Die before me then I will that the said Ten pounds shall go to & be paid to Her Eldest Daughter then living Also I give bequeath to my God daughter Elizabeth Gibson Daughter of William Gibson deceased the sum of Ten pounds And all this rest residue & remainder of my Goods Chattells Debts Rights Credit Moneys due by Mortgages as well such as and forfeited as are not forfeited Bonds & personall Estate whatsoever not herein before disposed of I give bequeath unto my said wife Elizabeth Read, And I do hereby make constitute & appoint my Trusty friends the said William Gale & Peter Gale Executors of this my last Will & Testament in Trust for the due perfect Execution thereof hereby revoking & making aside all former & other Wills & Testaments by me heretofore made & declaring *this & no other to being Last Will and Testament, in Witness whereof I have hereunto put my hand & seal the sixth day of October in the Year of our Lord One thousand seven hundred & forty seven*

Sealled published & declared in the presence of

November 6th 1747 Maths Read

Willm Jackson
Ann Hinde
J W Parkin

William Gale & Peter Gale sole executors in trust in this will named were sworn well & faithfully to execute & perform the same according to the Directions of the said will and so forth, before me Thos Sewell surrogate"

His will is lodged in the Lancashire County Record Office, Preston. Whitehaven used to fall within the Diocese of Chester and some of the records were passed to Lancashire.

46 Sir James Lowther as a boy, believed to be by Read (Holker Hall)

Whitehaven Painters

The number of artists who were born or lived in Whitehaven is impressive. The fact that they flourished and were noticed in the eighteenth century is partially due to the generally prosperous state of the town. As late as 1816 Whitehaven was recognised as the largest town in the north of England after Newcastle and York. Its population rose from 2,222 in 1693 to 9,063 in 1762 but it was not just the numbers of people which determined its status but the quality of life that was attained. Apart from the prospering commercial aspects there was a cultural side where music and the arts were appreciated, concerts were regularly held and a growing level of intellectual pursuits developed.

The main painters flourished between the following years:-

Mathias Read	*1669 - 1747*	
Joseph Hinde	*c. 1747 - 1762*	
Henry Hinde		
Strickland Lowry	*1737 - 1780*	*when he moved to Ireland*
Wilson Lowry	*1760 - 1824*	
Henry Nutter	*1758 - 1808*	*although he moved to Carlisle*
Matthew Wilkinson	*1773 - 1807*	*(in 1878 his work was recognised in a book published in America)*
Robert Salmon	*1775 - c.1844*	
John Clementson	*1780 - 1841*	*Married Frances Wilson Nov 5th 1816*
Joseph Heard	*1789 - 1859*	
Oliver Ullsinon (Hodgson)	*1830 - 1840*	
Henry Collins	*Married Elizabeth Hamilton, June 28th 1818*	
William Dougan	*Married Elizabeth Wilson, Widow*	

Eventually an Exhibition was launched in the nineteenth century with a sad result.

"The Whitehaven Artists Exhibition commenced its career, on Monday last under the auspices of Mr Johnson. We understand a tolerable collection of paintings. We hope that it will succeed; but we cannot help thinking that a more appropriate season of the year might be found than the very period when the Carlisle Academy is about to open".[75]

—less than three weeks later, there is another insertion:— "the Whitehaven Exhibition has, we are sorry to say, in one short season, terminated its career without a prospect of a revival. The receipts have been by no means equal to expenditure".[76]

Read's Paintings taken to Holker Hall.

Of the 162 pictures which were shipped from the Flatts to Holker in 1757, nine were listed as being by Read. "The Pictures taken on Acc' of & described by Joseph Hinde Painter: Packed up in 17 Cases or Boxes by Geo Hilton & ship'd on board the Prudence of Millthrop Lawrence Workington Master to be del'd to Mr William Richardson at Holker   *Sept 19th 1757"*

G F 2   *$^1/_2$ length (John Ld Viscount Lonsdale's) Lady by Read after Kneller.*

No.25   *$^3/_4$ length King William III by Read after Kneller.*

No.32   *$^3/_4$ length The Lady of John Lowther of Whitehaven by Read after Paert.*

No.33   *$^3/_4$ length Sir James Lowther, of Whitehaven, when young by Read after Kneller.*
       Illustration 46.

No.40   *$^3/_4$ length A Laughing Boy by Read after Scalkin. (Is now lost.)*

No.62   *Prospect of Lowther Hall by Read.*
       Colour Plate 7

No.66   *Copy of an Italian Landscape by Read after[77]*
       Illustration 4

No.71   *A Prospect of Whitehaven from Brackanthw't about ye yr 1730 by Read.*
       Colour Plate 12

No.80   *A Prospect of the inside of the Old Chapel at Whitehaven 1694. (probably by Read but not listed here as such)*

(Numbers preceding the pictures are taken from Hinde's list.)

Nos. 62 and 71 are still there, though no.80 the Prospect inside the Old Chapel is not. 66 and 25 are there but the latter is a small picture and not $^3/_4$ length as described on the list.

In the disastrous fire at Holker in 1871 about 103 of the total list were destroyed, and about "59 saved from the devouring element".[78]

In the published list of those destroyed No. 71 is described "Lady Lonsdale (Mary Lowther) – Reade, after Sir Godfrey Kneller", as the only Read destroyed.

In the list of paintings not destroyed made after the fire reference is made to two of Read's paintings – "53, William III - Reade, and 56 Whitehaven – Reade".

The identities of 2 and 32 still present problems.

The View of Whitehaven by Jan Wyck, a splendid early representation of Whitehaven from the sea signed 1686 is still at Holker hanging near to Read's Prospect of Whitehaven and the View of Lowther.

Colour Plate 1

A Prospect of Whitehaven

Line engraving by Richard Parr 1738-39

8" x 16¹/₂" (19.8 x 41.5 cms)

It would be helpful if there had been as much information about one single painting by Read as there is about the engraving by Richard Parr.

*A poster was printed to advertise a subscription towards **A Prospect of the Town and Harbour of Whitehaven** on 5th September 1738. The printer was Thomas Cotton of Whitehaven and the engraving was after one of the paintings by Mathias Read. The lively correspondence between James Spedding in London to his father John Spedding in Whitehaven (steward to Sir James Lowther) describes the flurry of excitement it caused in the town.*

The engraving was based on one of the versions of the painting of Whitehaven. His view includes the glasshouse, and Merchant's Quay so it rules out the two earlier versions. But it includes smoke and a little industrial complex which are not in the paintings. It raises the question is there a 5th picture done in between the first two and the second two, in about 1736. Daniel Hay in a letter of 8th September 1976 said "There may be a fourth version around somewhere" – and there was – perhaps there is yet another?

The print is probably closest to the Askham version which is the only one of the paintings with the ridge and furrow type ploughing lines in the foreground. Parr, if this is the case, has omitted many of the animals and figures and also added the ships in the bay and harbour. The Whitehaven and Askham pictures have the additional building near Holy Trinity Church, which is included in Parr's print. Although it is dated 1738 we know from the following records that it was more likely to be early in 1739.

Illustration 47.

The Spedding Letters.   *Carlisle Record Office.*

"*Sir James Lowther to John Spedding, London, 6 June 1732:*
    The picture of Whitehaven is well lik'd, I think to have a Print made of it,

Spedding to Lowther, Whitehaven, 11 June 1732:
    I am glad the picture of Whitehaven is so well liked, it would make a mighty handsome print and Mr Read tells me the printers would be so far from asking money for engraving it that they would give 8 or 10 guineas for the picture to engrave from it, but perhaps he is mistaken in his computation and I only mention it as his opinion.

Lowther to Spedding, London, 17 June 1732:
    Mr Read is much mistaken in his thinking that a printer would give anything for liberty to engrave and print the picture of Whitehaven for sale, for tho' it would make as pretty a print as most towns yet there would be but a small demand for it in regard to the country it is in. I must consider what good I can do by printing it myself and if I can oblige people or not by making them a present of it.

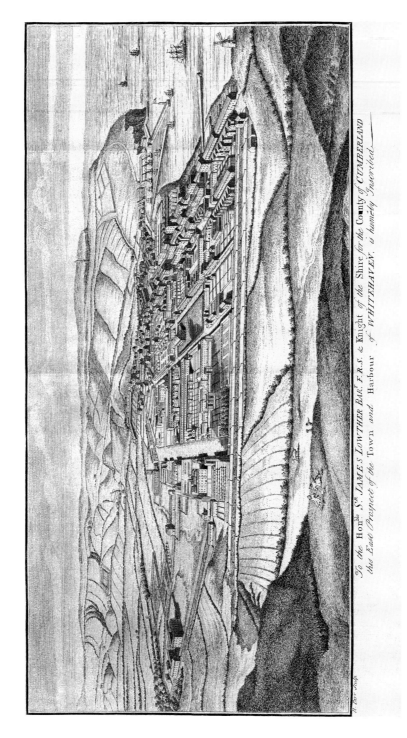

To the Honble Sr JAMES LOWTHER Bar.^t F.R.S. & Knight of the Shire for the County of CUMBERLAND
this East Prospect of the Town and Harbour of WHITEHAVEN, is humbly Inscribed.——

R. Parr Sculp

47 Richard Parr's print of Whitehaven

John Spedding to Sir James Lowther, Whitehaven, 29 Feb 1735 (-6):

Mr Read has finished the prospect of Whitehaven for Sir Thomas Lowther which much exceeds anything he did before. I suppose Sir Thomas will have it put up in a case and sent to Holker and shall wait his directions about it.

Spedding to Lowther, 10 Jan 1738 (-9)

By a short letter this post from poor James I find he is like to have a speedy call upon him from his engraver for more than his stock of cash will enable him to pay, wherefore I beg intreat your favour in supplying him with what his necessitys require, to the value of twenty or thirty pds if he wants it to carry on his prints of the town wch I shall thankfully make good to you.

Lowther to Spedding, London, 23 Jan 1738 (-9)

James has had vast trouble and spent a great deal of his time ever since he came to town about getting matters ready for the prints of Whitehaven, he has got the copper plates very well engraved and pretty reasonable but he has been sadly abused by a knavish stationer not only in the price of some of the paper but he has made it his business to sett the press maker and printer against him and had laid a wicked scheme to rob James of all the profit of his labour and industry to prevent which he is forced to be with the printer almost constantly from morning til evening otherwise he would print off so many for himself to sell at low prices for great profit that James might be a great looser.

Lowther to Spedding, London, 15 Feb 1738 (-9)

A letter expressing similar sentiments on the problems faced by James Spedding in getting the prints.

Lowther to Spedding, London, 27 Feb. 1738(-9)

He [James Spedding] has printed very near as many as he thinks he can get off, when I saw he was like to lose by having set them so low as three shillings I advised him to print a parcel at four shillings by which he will get ten pence a piece more than the others. What he writes of putting up his plates and prints at Whitehaven by way of lottery might engage him in more trouble and it is against an Act of Parliament tho' practiced here b some folks, It would not advise it but rather to keep his plates till he has sold his prints and then he may either print more or sell his plates.

Sir James Lowther to John Spedding, London, 7 Oct 1738

There is one objection to the dispersing so many prints to show the greatness and increase of buildings at Whitehaven which should be considered of, that is it may draw an increase of taxes on the town both for the Land tax and Window lights.

Same to Same, Same, 14 Oct 1738

James [Spedding] is vastly full about his print of Whitehaven. I wish the town does not suffer by dispersing too many. People take all advantages to squeeze money by taxes.

James Spedding in London to John Spedding in Whitehaven 7 November 1738[79]

I hope to have the Picture of Whitehaven soon, but can't make progress till then. Mr Fletcher from Holker tells me Sr Thomas has met with a misfortune. 40 gentlemen have subscribed there & this now makes a total of 300. More also from Mr & Mrs Ponsonby now about 400.

Mr Bucks tells me he can't positively say if he can begin the engraving as his brother has been delayed in going to Whitehaven, having had to do 2 prospects of Carlisle. He should be with you now but he seems honest & I hope the delay does not mean he will do one of Whitehaven himself. (They did do prospects of Carlisle, but the only prospect of Whitehaven in that period is Parr's. It begs the question did the Bucks withdraw from the engraving project, at some time before Parr took it on. At all events it would appear that the print did not finally appear until early in 1739.)"

48 Boar Hunt by Sawrey Gilpin

THE LAST BOAR HUNT. *by Sawrey Gilpin, 1733-1807*

Mr Kenneth Gilpin, Kentmere, Virginia, U S A.

Oil on board c.1750   48" x 48" (121.9 x 121.9 cms)

This is a classical scene of a boar hunt with one character attacking the boar. There are a number of early depictions of boar hunts dating from about 1300 onwards. The earliest example is of Roman date and carved in stone.

A boar is part of the arms of the Gilpin family and there is a legend that a Gilpin slew the last wild boar.

This painting was taken by the Gilpin family when they moved to Virginia, U S A in 1904. They named their new house there Scaleby after Scaleby Castle, Cumbria. **The Last Boar Hunt** *had hung at Scaleby Castle where William Gilpin (1657-1724) was Sir John Lowther's agent. William's son Captain John Bernard Gilpin (1701-1776) and his sons Sawrey and the Rev. William, also had their first lessons in art from Read, Capt. John said his happiest early memories were "to stand near Mr Read when he painted for his father".[80]*

As has already been mentioned Read certainly visited the Castle. Sawrey the grandson would have been a boy when he first met and was taught by Read and it is interesting to contemplate on whether he saw Read's version (now at Loweswater), of the **Last Boar Hunt** *as a young man. Sawrey was not born till 1733, while Read probably painted the Loweswater* **Last Boar Hunt** *in 1710 or shortly afterwards. In any case in 1747 Sawrey was apprenticed to Samuel Scott in Covent Garden where he lived till 1756.*

This was the period which influenced him strongly towards painting horses. He became one of Britain's leading horse painters. Indeed Stubbs, although eclipsing him, professed him to be his only rival! After his apprenticeship finished he stayed on till 1758 to assist Samuel Scott. His son William Sawrey Gilpin (1762-1843) held his first exhibition of water colours at the Royal Academy in 1797.

The Scaleby painting is quite different from the Read picture. It is a more sophisticated, realistic and well painted picture The dress shows a country squire in velvet sporting gear of about 1750. There is one dead hound and another that has been mauled by the boar. Three hounds are holding the boar and the rest of the hunt can be seen going off in the distance. Boar hunting was a very strenuous activity and used to encourage young men to be brave and strong.

The mouth and the eye of the boar are particularly detailed. Apart from the accuracy it is freely painted with much movement and conviction. Of particular interest is the little additional point common to both paintings, and what would suggest that Sawrey remembered Read's work. In both there is a small hollow tree stump with four projecting points. These bear no relation to the hunt but make one imagine that Sawrey, remembering Read's painting, included this purely in memory of Read's earlier work.

At Townend House, Troutbeck there is a small version in reverse of a similar scene.

Illustration 48.

Joseph Hinde. *by Joseph Hinde (1700?-1782)*   *James Cropper, Tolson Hall.*

Oil on canvas c.1743   14¹/4" x 11" (36 x 28 cms)

"Joseph Hinde of Tolson Hall Nr Kendal the great grandfather of Editha B H Bigland" is the inscription on the frame. Certainly this would appear to be Joseph the nephew of Mathias Read who married Elizabeth Hinde. There were two brothers Henry and Joseph and they were both painters. It was Joseph Hinde who made the list of paintings at Flatt Hall in 1757 one work listed was painted by him. He appeared to work from 1747-62 and were both probably born between 1700-1715 in Whitehaven. They lived in Cross Street, at No.5 which was bought by Margaret Gibson, after Read's death, a widow and possibly mother of Elizabeth Gibson, daughter of William. The former was Read's god-daughter. Margaret was the sister of Henry and Joseph who were the executors of her will. Joseph Hinde is mentioned in the 1762 Census as a painter. It is probable that Joseph provides a link between Read and later painters of the town.

*   **Strickland Lowry** was probably taught by Hinde. Strickland Lowry, born in Whitehaven, moved to Ireland in c.1762.*

*   The portrait is fresh and quite well painted. The hand holding a letter may have been of some significance, because Gibson was the postmaster and apparently features on a local Whitehaven poster about the introduction of the penny post. The only works to have survived by Joseph are copies of portraits in the Lowther collection.*

READ FAMILY TREE

WILLIAM REDE = HANNAH BLOUNT
1668 at St James Church, Clerkenwell

WILLIAM (REID)	WILLIAM	THOMAS	HANNAH
Baptised	*Bap. 6 Jan 1673*	*Bap. 28 Feb 1676*	*Bap. 1 Mar 1678*
15 Jul 1670	*at St James*	*at St James,*	*at St Vedast*
Died in infancy	*Clerkenwell*	*Clerkenwell*	*& St Michaels,*
			Le Querne, London

MATHIAS = ELIZABETH HINDE (*17 May 1702 at St Nicholas, Whitehaven*)
Born 1669Born 1668
Bap. 31 Dec 1671Daughter of Leonard & Margaret Hinde
at St James, Clerkenwell   of Prestonhowes, Whitehaven.
Died 8 Nov 1747Died 2 Apr 1748

WILLIAM READ	JANE	ELIZABETH
Born 3 Jul 1703	*Born 7 Jul 1705*	*Born 4 Apr 1707*
Died 7 Aug 1724	*Died 28 Mar 1722*	

Issue

THE FOUR TRUSTEES   *Private Collection.*

Oil on canvas. c.1730   49¹/₂" x 58¹/₂" (125.6 x 148.4 cms.)

From the painting of the faces this would appear to be by Read. The similarities of manner in the treatment of the faces in the group with Read's known portraits of William Gibson (Ill. 32) and Joseph Littledale (Ill. 35) are very strong. The picture was in the collection at Rydal Hall before the Hall was sold. The sitters from left to right are T. L. Parker of Browsholme; (The Parkers were intermarried with the family at Rydal Hall.) John, First Earl of Suffolk; Charles, Viscount Andover; Robert Rainsford.

This is the only known group portrait, which perhaps accounts for the rather random poses of the sitters.

Illustration 49.

49 The Four Trustees

FOOTNOTES

1   *Carlisle Library.*

2   *Whitehaven Library, Daniel Hay.*

3   *Industries in the Countryside. J. Thirsk, in F. J. Fisher (ed) Essays in the Economic & Social History of Tudor & Stuart England (Cambridge, 1961) p.86.*

4   *Pevsner, Cumberland and Westmorland, 1967, p.203.*

5   *Whitehaven 1660-1800. Sylvia Collier, London HMSO 1991, p.19.*

6   *ibid p.23.*

7   *'Coal & Tobacco' by J. V. Beckett, p.183, published by Cambridge University Press 1981.*

8   *op. cit. p.182.*

9   *Hutchinson, History of Cumberland, 1794, Vol. II, p.80.*

10 *Lowther Castle Sale 1947. (Catalogue 2, Lot 1895).*

11 *The National Gallery in Ireland has another version of the Battle of the Boyne dated 1693.*

12 *Correspondence of Sir John Lowther 1693-98. Edited by D. R. Hainsworth OUP, 1883, p.16.*

13 *W. Gilpin's Cash Accounts 1693-9, pp 18-20.*

14 *CCRO, Carlisle D/Lons/W3 W5.*

15 *John Harris, The Artist & the Country House. Sothebys Parke Bernet 1979, p.99. Read's Version at Tullie House Art Gallery.*

16 *Correspondence of Sir John Lowther 1693-98. Edited by D. R. Hainsworth OUP, 1883.*

17 *Information from the late Sylvia McCosh.*

18 *Eliane Gondinet-Wallstein. "Un retable pour l'Au-delà." Nouvelles Editions Mame. 1990.*

19 *CCRO, Carlisle D/Lons/W3 W5.*

20 *CCRO, Carlisle D/Lons/W Miscellaneous Colliery papers.*

21 *Cash Book: James Lowther No.7 Feb. 1722-Feb. 1725.*
    Jan. 5th 1725 By pd. Mr Read for copying ye map of Whitehaven 10/6
    Jan. 6th-20th 1724 by pd. Mr Read for painting ye Slaughter Ho door 17/6.

22 *The Rev. W. Gilpin, "Memoirs".*

23 *ibid.*

24 *William Jackson, Papers and Pedigrees, 1875.*

25 *CWAAS Transactions OS Vol. 3, 1878, p.347, 364-5.*

26 *Daniel Hay who was for many years Librarian at Whitehaven and wrote about Read: Cumbria 1973.*

27 *See Appendix I – indentures.*

28 *Mr Jackson records that it was not until 1728 that Read was called 'Mr' for the first time.*

29 *CCRO, Carlisle D/Lons/W3 W13 – "12 Sept. 1695: For painting an Interior Prospective of ye. New Church at Whitehaven - by direction of Sir John Lowther . . . 01.15.00.*

30 *Holy Trinity Vestry Book.*

31 *ibid.*

32 *ibid.*

33 *Humphrey Senhouse's Account Book for 30th July 1727 paid "Mr Smith the stone carver" ————" 9 days a cutting my dear son Jos. Richards upon marble with the Senhouse coat-of-arms and an inscription of about 240 letters — "*
    "D O M
    Hic requiescit Jofephus Richardus Senhouse Humfreai Senhouse armi & Eleanore Conjugis Filius Natu maximus formce decore ingenioq infignis Cuinec viventi generosa virtus nec morienti vera pietas defuir Vixit ans XIX mens Vidies XV
    Obijt die XI Decembris MDCCCXVIII"

34 *Appendix II.*

35 *J. Walker, History of Penrith from the Earliest Period to the Present Time, 1858.*

36 *Hutchinson, History of Cumberland, Vol. I p.323-324.*

37 *Appendix II.*

38 *William Furness, History of Penrith from the Earliest Record to the Present Time 1894.*

39 *For the translation of Dr Brownrigg's medical report grateful thanks to Mrs Jean Ward and Dr Joan Yell.*

40 *Dr Brownrigg (1711-1801)* left detailed accounts of his work in Whitehaven which are being carefully edited by Mrs Ward and Dr Yell.*
   *His birth was registered as 1711 which was according to the old calendar, in modern times it would be 1712.

41 *Later, others were sent which made the total 162, see Paintings still at Holker.*

42 *E. H. Gombrich, Art & Illusion, Phaidon, 1959.*

43 *Prospects of Town & Park, Catalogue, Colnaghi 1988 Intro. John Harris, Exhib. to mark 85th birthday of NACF.*

44 *John Harris, The Artist & the Country House, Sothebys, 1979.*

45 *Sir Kenneth Clark, Landscape in Art (John Murray, London 1976).*

46 *J. Ruskin, The Works III pp.623-4.*

47 *CWAAS Transactions NS 1921 p.180.*

48 *M.W. Taylor, M.D. CWAAS Extra Series Vol.VIII, 1892, p.294.*

49 *CWAAS Transactions OS VIII 1886 p.477. The picture referred to here is probably the same and was extant in the Abbey in 1886; CWAAS Transactions NS 1953 pp. 81-97.*

50 *John Harris, The Artist & the Country House. Sothebys, 1979.*

51 *CWAAS Transactions NS LXI 1961 p.212.*

52 *Clerk of Penicuick papers, Box 82/2109, Edinburgh Record Office.*

53 *CWAAS Transactions NS LXI p.212.*

54 *Personal correspondence with Mary Wane of Windermere for access to her current research into her family.*

55 *In James Clarke's Survey of the Lakes of Cumberland, Westmorland and Lancashire, 1787.*

56 *The picture may have been commissioned by the owner of the Grapes, a house seen in a drawing by W. H. Nutter **Market Place**, Tullie House Art Gallery.*

57 *John Harris – The Artist & the Country House, Sothebys, 1979, p.99.*

58 *Letter to Mr Hay from Richard Cavendish 6th Sept 1978, Whitehaven Library.*

59 *Holker Archives – List of pictures at Flatt Hall.*

60 *'An Account of the Coal Mines' by Brownrigg, published 1801 and written by Joshua Dixon from Brownrigg's notes.*

61 *Personal communication from Ian Kyle.*

62 *C. Caine, The Churches of Whitehaven Rural Deanery, Halton & Sons, 1916. Caine also refers to a painting of Parton which was extant in 1916. He describes how the railway now runs over the buried harbour. This could be the painting to which he refers.*

63 *J.V. Becket, Coal & Tobacco, Cambridge, 1981, Beckett, pp 46, 50 & 164.*

64 *op. cit. p.137.*

65 *Miss Peile, Nineteenth Century Diary, still held in the family.*

66 *Abbot Hall Art Gallery, 1982, "Four Hundred Years of Cumbrian Painting" Cat.No.11.*

67 *It so happened that one of the authors had noticed a painting in a friend's house. The likeness of the two was so remarkable that it seemed fair to assume on stylistic grounds that they were by the same hand. In the second picture the boy holds the head of a greyhound with his right hand, his left resting on his hip. The other picture shows the boy in the opposite stance, left hand on an identical dog and right, on his hip.*

68 *Hilda Gamlin.*

69 *Encyclopaedia Judaica, Published by Kellel, New York.*

70 *B. L. Thompson, Royal Arms in the Diocese of Carlisle, CWAAS Transactions NS 1969.*

71 *N. Harris, verbal communication.*

72 *Grapes Inn (Read Murals)*
   Carlisle Journal 4 April 1873 –
   Grapes Inn offered or sale and bought along with the whole lane by the City (they intended to demolish part of the lane).

   Carlisle Journal 14 May 1880 – Town Council proceedings:

Matthias Read paintings in Old Grapes Hotel should be in care of Corporation "Mr Ferguson said the landlord rather objected in having them removed before the Royal Show (held in city in 1880) as being on panel their removal would cause some confusion".

Carlisle Journal 31 December 1880 –

Details of paintings of Carlisle and Whitehaven recently cleaned by Messrs Thurnam.

undated cutting at back of A53. Jackson Collection, Carlisle Library (obviously of 1880)

"Carlisle Corporation pictures - there are now on view in Messrs Thurnams Gallery three curious pictures, the property of the Corporation of Carlisle which will shortly be placed in the Town Hall. There is every reason to believing that they are the productions of Matthias Read . . . the pictures in question were formerly in the Old Grapes Inn, but have been taken out and cleverly cleaned by Messrs Thurnam of the thick coats of varnish, smoke and dust which covered them."

Carlisle Journal 17 May 1898 local jottings

"Town Hall paintings cleaned – much cleaner"

Alas there is the proof of the paint having been lifted as the coats of varnish, smoke and dust were removed.

73 *The Medical Casebook of William Brownrigg, M.D., F.R.S., (1712-1800) of the town of Whitehaven in Cumberland. Edited and translated by Jean Ward and Joan Yell.*
    Medical History Supplement no. 133. 1993. Welcome Institute for the History of Medicine, London..

74 *Ellis Waterhouse, The Dictionary of British Eighteenth Century painters, Antique Collectors Club 1981.*

75 *Carlisle Journal, 2 September 1826.*

76 *Carlisle Journal, 29 September 1826.*

77 *Mr Hay omits the Italian landscape from his list but includes the Holy family by Carracci which was in the possession of the Gilpin family and in the Scaleby sale of 1904.*

78 *Cumberland Pacquet: 17 March 1871 and 12 Sept. 1826.*

79 *Wordsworth Museum Trust.*

80 *The Rev. W. Gilpin "Memoirs".*

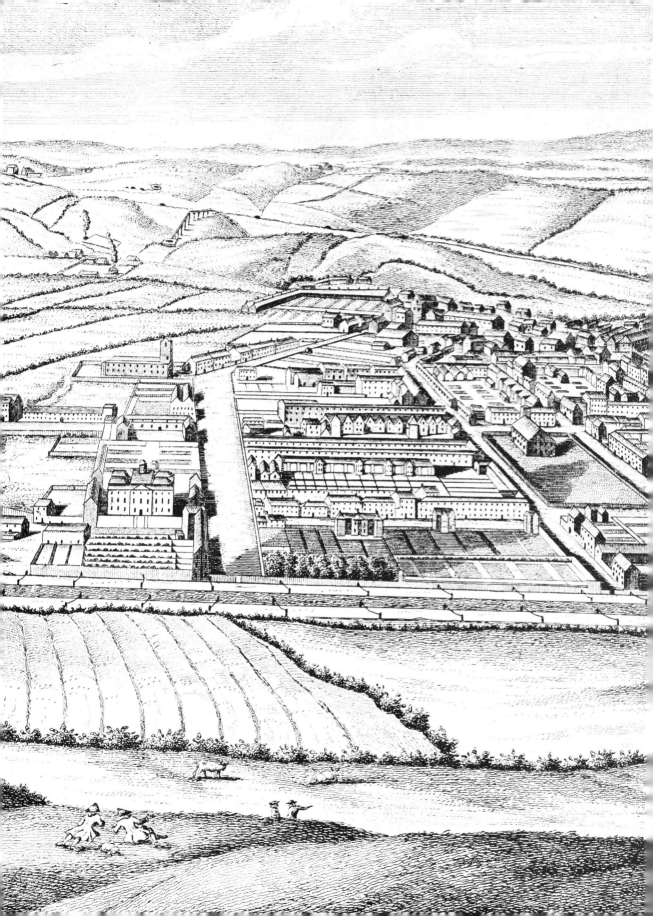